# Mission-Critical Governance

Corporate governance is failing—not because boards lack intelligence, experience, or diligence, but because the systems they rely on no longer surface the information that truly matters.

Across industries and jurisdictions, boards approve strategies, review risk lists, receive assurance reports, and comply with governance codes—yet remain blindsided by catastrophic failures. Safety collapses. Cultural scandals erupt. Financial integrity breaks down. Courts increasingly ask the same question after the fact: *Why didn't the board know?*

*Mission-Critical Governance* exposes the root cause of this failure: Boards govern without a clearly defined purpose and without reliable oversight of the mission-critical objectives (MCOs) that determine enterprise survival and success.

Drawing on decades of governance practice, landmark court decisions, behavioural science, and emerging regulatory expectations, this book challenges the dominant "checklist" model of governance and replaces it with a new architecture built for uncertainty. It introduces a practical, evidence-based framework that enables boards to:

- define and disclose board purpose with clarity and accountability;
- identify and oversee **MCOs**;
- quantify and report uncertainty using **Acceptable/Unacceptable Uncertainty** thresholds;
- measure confidence in information through the **Board Assurance Index (BAI)**;
- integrate risk, assurance, culture, and performance into a single oversight system; and
- break the destructive *Don't Tell/Don't Ask* governance syndrome.

This is not a compliance manual. It is a redesign of governance itself—from ritual to responsibility, from risk lists to real oversight, and from comfort to confidence.

Written for board directors, executives, regulators, investors, auditors, and risk leaders, *Mission-Critical Governance* provides a clear roadmap for transforming governance into a disciplined, purpose-anchored system capable of earning trust, withstanding scrutiny, and guiding organizations through an era of relentless uncertainty.

The question is no longer whether boards must govern differently.

The question is whether they will lead—or wait for courts, crises, and capital markets to force the change.

**Security, Audit and Leadership Series**
*Series Editor: Dan Swanson, Dan Swanson and Associates, Ltd., Winnipeg, Manitoba, Canada.*

**About the Book Series**
The scope and mandate for cybersecurity and internal audit continues to evolve each year, as does the complexity of the business environment and speed of the changing risk landscape in which it must operate. The fundamental goal of this exciting series is to produce leading-edge books on critical subjects facing security and audit executives and practitioners. Key topics addressed include Leadership, Cybersecurity, Security Leadership, Privacy, Strategic Risk Management, Auditing IT and Technology, and Audit Management and Leadership.

**If you're interested in submitting a proposal for a book to be included in the series, please email the series editor, Dan Swanson: dswanson_2008@yahoo.ca**

**Relevant Impact:** A Field Guide to Integrated Assurance
*By Patrick M. Hayes*

**Cybersecurity and the Art of Cyberwar**
*By Dan Shoemaker, Tamara Shoemaker, and Amir Jabri*

**Trust Hacked:** *What Firewalls, Failures, and the Frontlines Taught Me About Trust*
*By Nia Luckey*

**Organizational Resilience & Artificial Intelligence:** *A Practical Framework for Crisis Leadership, Adaptability & Sustainable Performance*
*By Arnab Mukherjee and Sachin Kumar*

**Mission-Critical Governance:** *Focusing on What Matters Most*
*By Tim J. Leech*

# Mission-Critical Governance

## Focusing on What Matters Most

Tim J. Leech

CRC Press
Taylor & Francis Group
Boca Raton London New York

CRC Press is an imprint of the
Taylor & Francis Group, an **informa** business

Designed cover image: Shutterstock ID: 1557677603

First edition published 2027
by CRC Press
2385 NW Executive Center Drive, Suite 320, Boca Raton FL 33431

and by CRC Press
4 Park Square, Milton Park, Abingdon, Oxon, OX14 4RN

*CRC Press is an imprint of Taylor & Francis Group, LLC*



ISBN: 9781041166658 (hbk)
ISBN: 9781041166665 (pbk)
ISBN: 9781003685753 (ebk)

DOI: 10.1201/9781003685753

Typeset in Caslon
by Newgen Publishing UK

# Contents

# About the Author

**Tim J. Leech**, FCPA, FCA is Founder and Managing Director of Risk Oversight Solutions, Inc. He is a leading authority on board governance, fiduciary oversight, and cost-effective enterprise risk and assurance. He has advised boards and senior executives around the world for over four decades, with a particular focus on how directors oversee strategy, assurance, mission-critical objectives, risk, and uncertainty. His articles on board risk oversight have been featured in *Harvard Law Forum on Governance*, *Conference Board Director Notes*, *Handbook of Board Governance*, *Cyber Risk Handbook*, *Ethical Boardroom*, *Columbia Law*, *London School of Economics*, *Strategic Finance*, *IIA Magazine*, and many others.

Tim is widely recognized for advancing *Purpose-Driven Governance* and *Objective-Centric Risk & Uncertainty Management*, practical frameworks designed to address recurring board oversight and accountability governance failures. In addition to his advisory work, he has been engaged as an **expert forensic accountant/governance witness** in cases involving alleged **officer/director negligence, and a wide range of civil and criminal matters.**

Tim is a former senior audit and risk executive, C&L Control & Risk Management Services practice director, founder and CEO of CARDdecisions, and author of CARDmap, the world's first integrated risk and assurance software. Tim is a Fellow of the Chartered Professional Accountants of Ontario (FCPA/FCA). He has been recognized for outstanding contributions to the CA/CPA profession, IIA, Certified Fraud Examiners, and the Center for Ethics and Corporate Governance. He is widely recognized as one of the top GRC trainers in the world. He provides training directly to companies around the globe, and virtually 24/7 via c-Risk Academy (https://criskacademy.teachable.com/p/cmora). He was engaged by Credit Institute of Canada in winter of 2022 to design and teach their first ever graduate-level course—Credit Risk Management Through an Objectives and Performance Lens. His third class just graduated.

He is married to Elaine, has two daughters and three grandchildren. His eldest daughter served in CAE and CRO roles, but left those professions because they were increasingly being marginalized to roles that add little value (risk list ERM/SOX support). He lives in Oakville, Ontario, Canada.

# Author's Note and Use of AI

This book represents the culmination of more than four decades of work around the globe in governance, risk, and assurance—work shaped by thousands of conversations with directors, executives, regulators, auditors, and risk professionals around the world.[1] The concepts of Purpose-Driven Governance (PDG), Objective-Centric Risk & Uncertainty Management (OCRUM), Mission-Critical Objectives (MCOs), and the "Don't Tell/Don't Ask Governance Syndrome" (DT/DA GS) have emerged from real-world experience, hard-won lessons, and a deep conviction that corporate governance can—and must—do better.

Although I am the author of this book, I did not write every sentence by hand. Like many authors today, I used a combination of my own experience and research, prior writings, extensive notes, and modern tools—including advanced AI—to help research, draft, refine, and structure the material.[2] But the ideas, frameworks, arguments, and conclusions are entirely my own. During the research phase, ChatGPT absorbed tens of thousands of pages of my posts, articles, presentations, and training aids/books, and completed thousands of research probes on governance-related questions. Although AI helped, every chapter in this book reflects core insights, positions, and language I have developed and championed for decades.

AI served here not as a creator of ideas but as a powerful amplifier—helping me express long-held frameworks and views with greater clarity, coherence, and reach. I reviewed, revised, and approved every concept, every message, and every word. The intellectual ownership of this work rests with me alone.

I am grateful to the colleagues, critics, and supporters including over 13,500 LinkedIn followers who—over many years—challenged my thinking and strengthened these ideas. Particular thanks go to Bruce McCuaig. Bruce was General Auditor at Gulf Canada where we proposed and successfully launched objective centric control and risk management self-assessment in mid 1980s, and my human behaviour advisory team—Dr. Karl O'Sullivan, Dr. Steve Swallow, and Dr. Dennis Fisher—who helped me understand human dynamics, particularly those related to what I have labelled DT/DA GS that a majority of organizations today have. While technology has made the writing process faster, the substance of this book has been shaped by human experience, human failures, and human aspirations for better governance and a better future. Special thanks to my wife Elaine, daughters, Morgan and Lauren, and partners Jamie and Niall who have had to contend with years of what many might see as obsessive research, posts, articles, and advocacy work on social media.

My hope is that this book does more than diagnose what is broken/sub-optimal. I hope it gives leaders the courage, tools, and clarity to build something better: governance with purpose, risk/uncertainty oversight with integrity, more fulfilling jobs for risk and internal audit professionals, and boardroom culture that seeks truth to guide decisions instead of comforting illusion.

## Notes

1 An overview of companies and countries the author has provided services to is available at https://riskoversightsolutions.com/about-us/

2 Drafting and analysis were supported by ChatGPT5 (OpenAI), a large language model–based AI tool, and AI tools accessed using Google Chrome browser. For ChatGPT approximately 84% of sessions were GPT-5.2, 15% were GPT-5.2 (auto-thinking variant), ~1% were GPT-5.1. Chrome browser uses Gemini and other AI engines. Final judgements and conclusions are the author's.

# Quick Reference Glossary

### The Core Model

- MCO(s) (Mission-Critical Objective(s)): The few objectives that determine success, survival, and stakeholder trust.
- OCRUM (Objective-Centric Risk & Uncertainty Management): Managing uncertainty in relation to specific objectives—not generic risk lists.
- PDG (Purpose-Driven Governance): Governance anchored in a clearly defined board purpose, focused on what matters most.

### How Boards Evaluate Risk and Confidence

- AU/UU (Acceptable/Unacceptable Uncertainty): This is the level of uncertainty linked to an objective acceptable to the board.
- BAI (Board Assurance Index): A simple rating of how confident the board is in the reliability of information it receives.

How Assurance Works

- IOCA (Integrated Objective-Centric Assurance): Aligns internal audit, risk, compliance, and external assurance around MCOs.

The Core Governance Failure

- DT/DA GS (Don't Tell/Don't Ask Governance Syndrome): Management doesn't tell. Boards don't ask. Critical risks stay hidden.

Legacy System (What This Book Replaces)

- ERM (Enterprise Risk Management): Traditional approach using risk registers and heat maps—often disconnected from objectives.

# PART I

# The Governance Illusion

## How Boards Lost Their Purpose

# 1
# The Purpose Void

*When purpose is unclear, governance becomes an exercise in ritual compliance theatre.*

## 1.1 Introduction: The Great Drift

Modern corporate governance did not collapse in one dramatic moment; it simply **drifted off course**.

Over decades, boards of directors came to equate "good governance" with *process adherence*—review of management's annual strategic plan and quarterly progress reports, internal audit plans proposed and completed, lists of "top risks" and "risk heatmaps," policies approved, meetings held—while forgetting that those rituals were never the destination. They were meant to serve a higher end: *the sustained achievement of the organization's purpose and supporting objectives.*

The drift is subtle but pervasive. Every code, regulation, and professional standard claim to strengthen governance, yet almost none define *why* governance exists—its' purpose. The result is a paradox: Compliance indicators rise, while public trust and corporate resilience fall. This vacuum—the **Purpose Void**—is the silent fault line beneath every subsequent chapter of this book.

## 1.2 The Missing Definition of Governance Purpose

As shown in Table 1.1 no global standard yet tells directors or stakeholders, in precise terms, what the *purpose of governance itself* is.

Without that anchor, boards interpret purpose through whatever lens dominates the moment—shareholder primacy, stakeholder balance, ESG reputation, or regulatory avoidance.

DOI: 10.1201/9781003685753-2

**Table 1.1** Comparative Definition Gap

| FRAMEWORK/JURISDICTION | MENTIONS "PURPOSE" | DEFINES PURPOSE OF GOVERNANCE | DEFINES PURPOSE OF THE BOARD | STATUS |
|---|---|---|---|---|
| Delaware DGCL[a]/Caremark line | Implied (shareholder value) | NO | NO | Legal precedent, not definition |
| UK Corporate Governance Code[b] (2024) | ✓ (corporate purpose) | NO | NO | "Principle B" p.6 urges alignment but gives no test |
| OECD Principles[c] (2023) | ✓ | NO | NO | States boards *should promote long-term interests* |
| ISO 37000[d] (2021) | ✓ ("purpose of the organization") | NO | NO | Avoids prescribing board-level purpose |
| King IV/V[e] (South Africa, 2016/2025) | ✓✓ | ✓ (for organization) | Partial | Closest, but still not very clear |

Notes:

[a] Delaware General Corporations Law: https://delcode.delaware.gov/title8/c001/

[b] UK Governance Code 2024/effective 2025: www.frc.org.uk/library/standards-codes-policy/corporate-governance/uk-corporate-governance-code/

[c] G20 OECD Principles of Corporate Governance 2023: www.oecd.org/en/topics/policy-issues/corporate-governance.html

[d] ISO 37000 2021, Governance of Organizations, Corporate Governance: https://committee.iso.org/ISO_37000_Governance

[e] King V Code on Corporate Governance for South Africa 2025: www.iodsa.co.za/resource/collection/927F0970-C1E9-4F30-803C-D74BF386A2B6/King_V_Code.pdf

## 1.3 How We Got Here

### *1.3.1 From Stewardship to Compliance*

Corporate boards were born to represent owners and oversee *purposeful stewardship*. Early charters spoke of "public benefit," "sound management," and "trusteeship." Over time, litigation fear and bureaucratic layering shifted the objective from **achieving purpose** to **avoiding blame**.

The "business judgment rule," originally meant to encourage initiative, mutated into a defensive shield.

### *1.3.2 The Metrics Takeover*

In the 1990s, the rise of internal-control frameworks and audit-centric ratings made governance measurable—but only in mechanical unreliable ways. Boxes ticked became proof of diligence. Yet subjective opinions on **internal control effectiveness** is not the same as **strategic confidence/acceptable risk**. As Peter Senge warned in his seminal book on organizational learning, systems optimized for measurement often suppress learning.[1]

### *1.3.3 The Silence of the Codes*

Each new reform—Sarbanes-Oxley, UK Combined Code, US Dodd-Frank, Corporate Sustainability Reporting Directive (CSRD)—promised transparency. Few asked whether the data flowing upward actually answered what should be the board's fundamental question: *Are we on track to achieve our purpose?* None required boards to define that purpose first.

## 1.4 The Symptoms of a Purpose Void

1. **Procedural Proliferation**—growing volume of checklists with shrinking insight.
2. **Fragmented Accountability**—staff functions, not management, "own" risk, internal control, and compliance, leaving boards passive.

3. **Short-Term Myopia**—quarterly optics eclipse mission-critical endurance.
4. **Semantic Fog**—terms like "risk appetite," "value," "internal control effectiveness", and "assurance" used without shared meaning.
5. **Trust Erosion**—stakeholders sense governance theatre, not real board engagement.

Boards rarely notice these symptoms until failure exposes them. By then, reputational damage is irreversible, and regulators add still more process, with little or no real attempt to study if those processes actually accomplish intended purpose—deepening the void.

### 1.5 The Economic Scale of the Problem

The Purpose Void is not philosophical—it is expensive. McKinsey's long-term data on listed-company life expectancy shows average tenure on major indices collapsing from 60 years (1960) to under 18 years today.[2] Studies of major collapses—Boeing, Wells Fargo, Wirecard, Carillion, 2008 Global Financial Crisis —reveal governance systems that looked compliant until they imploded.

ChatGPT estimates direct value destruction from governance-related failures in the past four decades exceeds **one quadrillion US dollars** globally when cumulative market, pension, social-trust losses, and missed opportunities are combined.[3] That figure—staggering but conservative—is why this book frames the issue as *the Quadrillion-Dollar Question.*

### 1.6 Why Boards Avoid Defining Board Purpose

1. **Ambiguity Feels Safe.** A vague charter offends no constituency.
2. **Fear of Measurement.** A clear purpose invites performance tests.
3. **Fragmented Ownership.** Directors see entity purpose as management's job; management sees it as branding.
4. **Liability Concerns.** Board purpose statements could be discoverable in court.

5. **Cognitive Dissonance.** Admitting uncertainty threatens personal competence narratives.

This avoidance culture is the seedbed of *Don't Tell/Don't Ask* Governance covered in Chapter 2. When the top of the organization cannot define success, every function below optimizes for survival instead of contribution.

### 1.7 How Purpose Drift Erodes Risk and Assurance

Without a declared board purpose:

- **Risk functions** chase regulatory and/or board-required risk lists and "principal risks" (e.g.UK Governance Code paragraph 28), rather than helping those responsible for objectives manage uncertainty so that key objectives will be achieved with a level of risk/uncertainty acceptable to the CEO and the board.
- **Internal audit** reports management's "internal control deficiencies/weaknesses" divorced from mission relevance and performance (compliance/process/controls focus).
- **Boards** drown in metrics that do not answer whether the enterprise is succeeding and whether level of risk/uncertainty being accepted is acceptable to the board (objectives-centric focus).

The more data generated, the less meaning boards extract. Quantity masquerades as assurance.

### 1.8 Reclaiming Purpose as the Governance North Star

Every governance system that works begins with an explicit, collective understanding of *why the organization exists* and *how success will be known.*

Entity Purpose is not a slogan; it is a set of **mission-critical objectives (MCOs)** that can be achieved or missed.

Re-anchoring governance to purpose requires three assertions:

1. **Purpose Precedes Strategy.** Strategy is simply purpose in motion.
2. **Purpose Demands Measurement.** If it cannot be observed, it cannot be overseen.

3. **Purpose Requires Dialogue.** Clarity on big picture purpose needs to guide strategy.

### 1.9 The Bridge to Purpose-Driven Governance (PDG)

PDG re-frames the board's purpose, its raison d'etre:

- **Define/Refine** the organization's purpose in explicit, verifiable terms.
- **Oversee defining/executing** MCOs that make that purpose real.
- **Oversee** uncertainty/risk linked to each MCO.
- **Assure** the board's confidence using integrated evidence.

PDG does not add new bureaucracy; it replaces diffuse oversight with disciplined clarity.

### 1.10 Case Snapshot: When Purpose Is Clear

Consider two anonymized multinationals of similar scale.

- Company A (a composite drawn from multiple real-world governance transformations) defined its core purpose—"advancing sustainable mobility"—and linked executive pay, risk reporting, and assurance directly to five MCOs. Over five years it reduced surprise losses > 60%.
- **Company B** maintained generic governance processes with no explicit purpose linkage. When a product-safety failure hit, siloed reports delayed action by months, wiping out $18 billion in market value.

The difference was not ethics or talent. It was *clarity*.

### 1.11 Why PDG Is Different

Traditional reforms fix symptoms—new committees, disclosures, or certifications.[4] PDG fixes **cause**.

It restores a hierarchy long inverted:

**Purpose → Objectives → Uncertainty → Assurance → Confidence.** Everything else—codes, audits, frameworks—belongs beneath that chain. Once purpose is defined, uncertainty can be measured; once uncertainty is measured, assurance has meaning; once assurance has meaning, boards earn confidence they are fulfilling board purpose.

### 1.12 Implications for Boards, Regulators, and Investors

- **Boards** must evidence purpose alignment in decisions and disclosures.
- **Regulators** should evaluate governance quality by clarity of board purpose and how it is being fulfilled, not volume of board procedures.
- **Investors** should price governance quality by demonstrated board oversight of MCOs, risk/uncertainty linked to MCOs, and performance.

Purpose thus becomes a **market signal**, not a public-relations line.

### 1.13 From Void to Voice: The Next Question

The remaining chapters trace how the Purpose Void enabled the cultural silence now entrenched in many institutions. Understanding that silence—*the Don't Tell/Don't Ask Governance Syndrome*—is the next step.

*If governance cannot speak its purpose, it cannot hear the truth.*

### Notes

1 The Fifth Discipline: The Art & Practice of the Learning Organization, Peter M. Senge (1990).

2 Why you will probably live longer than most big companies, IMD, 2016: www.imd.org/research-knowledge/disruption/articles/why-you-will-probably-live-longer-than-most-big-companies/#:~:text=A%20recent%20study%20by%20McKinsey,%2C%20Alphabet%2C%20Microsoft%20or%20Amazon.

3 Research done by ChatGPT in 2025 in response to research requests for Tim Leech to estimate the cumulative cost of preventable governance failures in terms of direct value destruction, including lost opportunities.

4 For an analysis of regulatory responses to multiple waves of governance disasters see Preventing the next wave of unreliable financial reporting: Why US Congress should amend Section 404 of the Sarbanes – Oxley Act Tim J. Leech, Lauren Hanlon, *International Journal of Disclosure and Governance* 2011: https://riskoversightsolutions.com/wp-content/uploads/2022/07/Open-Paper-LL-Why-US-Congress-Should-Amend-SO.pdf

# 2 DON'T TELL/DON'T ASK GOVERNANCE SYNDROME

*Silence is rarely neutral. In governance, it has often been what isn't said that's key.*

## 2.1 Introduction: The Psychology of Silence

Every governance failure begins with a silence that seemed harmless at the time.

Someone knew but didn't say. Someone suspected but didn't ask.

Over months and years those tiny acts of self-protection harden into a system of avoidance that looks professional but feels sterile. It has rituals, metrics, and minutes—but no truth.

This is the behavioural root of the **Don't Tell/Don't Ask (DT/DA) Syndrome**.

It is not a conspiracy but a choreography: Executives learn what the board prefers not to hear, and boards learn how to interpret vagueness as reassurance.

Everyone stays comfortable; nobody stays informed.

PDG names this pattern for what it is—a **governance defence mechanism** masquerading as diligence.

Until boards understand *why* they (management/boards) collectively choose silence, technical reforms will only decorate the problem.

DOI: 10.1201/9781003685753-3

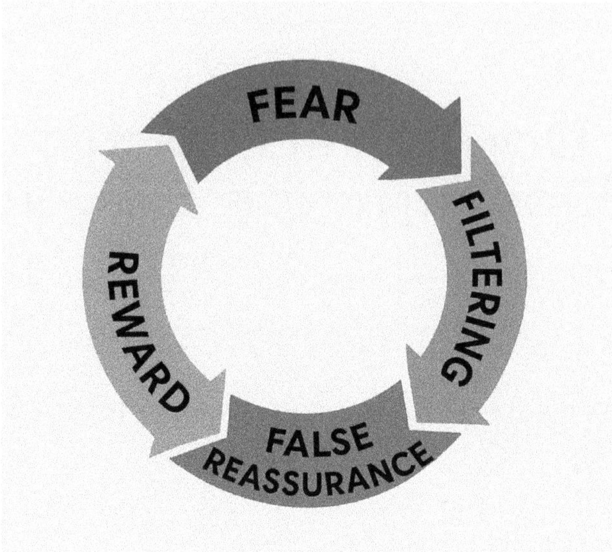


**Figure 2.1** The Information Suppression Cycle.

## 2.2 The Anatomy of DT/DA

At its simplest, the cycle works like this (see Figure 2.1):

1. **Fear of Punishment or Embarrassment.** Managers hesitate to surface uncertainty or bad news.
2. **Filtering and Re-framing.** Data are softened to match expectations; metrics are "managed."
3. **False Reassurance.** Boards interpret the absence of red flags as evidence of control.
4. **Reward and Reinforcement.** Calm meetings and "no surprises" bonuses reinforce the behaviour.
5. **Renewed Fear.** Speaking up later becomes even riskier.

Round after round, the system grows quieter—and apparently more successful—until it isn't.

## 2.3 Behavioural Drivers and Reinforcers

These are not moral failings; they are *adaptive behaviours* to the environment the company and board itself design (see Table 2.1).

**Table 2.1** Behavioural Drivers and Reinforcers

| DRIVER | TYPiCAL EXPRESSION | REINFORCING MECHANISM |
|---|---|---|
| **Status Preservation** | Executives curate information to protect perceived competence. | Performance appraisals reward composure, not candour. |
| **Group Conformity** | Directors mirror one another's optimism to maintain cohesion. | Social belonging outweighs intellectual dissent. |
| **Reciprocal Politeness** | "You don't challenge me; I don't challenge you." | Courtesy becomes collusion. |
| **Ambiguity Comfort** | Vague goals allow multiple self-justifying narratives. | Everyone can claim success. |
| **Fear of Liability** | Caution about minutes or discovery suppresses inquiry. | Legal counsel's shadow shapes discussion tone. |
| **Time Compression** | Overloaded agendas leave no space for uncertainty. | Efficiency theatre replaces exploration. |

Change the environment—reward curiosity, protect dissent, measure confidence—and behaviour follows.

### 2.4 How Culture Sanitizes Information

The DT/DA dynamic thrives where organizations worship *professional calm.*

When the signal of competence is the ability to stay unruffled, data that might disturb equilibrium are automatically muted.

Language becomes the lubricant of denial: "variance," "timing issue," "isolated control gap."

Boards unknowingly encourage this by demanding "executive summaries" instead of evidence.

The thicker the summary, the thinner the insight.

A director rarely intends to suppress truth; they simply act within norms that equate questioning with conflict.

The consequence is a **self-curated reality**—an echo chamber in which everything sounds fine until external stakeholders speak louder or a corporate governance disaster becomes public.

### 2.5 Case Snapshot: Bank Alpha

Bank Alpha (fictionalized composite from author's client experience) prided itself on "no-surprise governance."

Quarterly packs ran 400 pages yet contained not one explicit statement about risk linked to mission-critical objectives.

When a massive trading-desk loss finally surfaced, directors were stunned: "How could we not have known?"

The answer: they had *known* pieces of it all along, but no single meeting ever connected them.

The bank's culture rewarded certainty; analysts who modelled worst-case exposures were branded pessimists.

After the loss, an internal review found multiple clues, each toned down after management review.

No individual lied; the *system edited itself.*

### 2.6 Why Rational People Participate

Classical economics and logic assume rational actors seek truth to optimize outcomes.

Behavioural governance shows the opposite: people often seek *psychological safety* over accuracy.[1]

In boardrooms, the **fear of looking ignorant** exceeds the fear of being ignorant.

Directors hesitate to ask basic questions ("What could go wrong?") lest they appear untrusting/uninformed.

Executives reciprocate by over-simplifying, reinforcing directors' illusion of understanding.

Thus, DT/DA isn't driven by deceit but by **ego-risk management**—the quiet protection of self-image.

### 2.7 Illustrative Fictional Case Snapshot: Manufacturer Beta

Manufacturer Beta had a celebrated safety record and glossy sustainability reports. Internally, a design flaw had been flagged three times by engineers, each time framed as "performance variance." Middle managers feared that the admission might delay a flagship product launch tied to executive bonuses.

When the defect finally triggered a recall, the board asked why its Audit and Risk Committees had never seen it. The answer mirrored Bank Alpha's: *every layer believed someone above them already knew.* DT/DA is not concealment; it is **distributed assumption of disclosure**.

After the crisis, an independent review mapped more than 60 separate reporting artefacts touching safety risk—none of which required an explicit statement of *confidence that the mission-critical objective—safe launch—remains on track.*

The information system produced noise, not knowledge.

### 2.8 Behavioural Archetypes inside DT/DA

Drawing on decades of research in groupthink, cognitive bias, and organizational silence, five recurring boardroom behaviours witnessed by the author in hundreds of board packs consistently suppress early warning signals:

1. **The Optimist** frames uncertainty as opportunity, convinced positivity sustains morale.
2. **The Interpreter** edits or reframes bad news to align with "the narrative."
3. **The Deflector** diverts questions to technical detail, exhausting inquiry.
4. **The Peacekeeper** discourages challenge to preserve board harmony.
5. **The Historian** reminds everyone that "we've seen this before and it worked out."

These archetypes coexist peacefully until a trigger event—a loss, scandal, or whistleblower—breaks the illusion. The moment after the illusion shatters is often described as *shock*, but it is actually **cognitive debt repayment**: the accumulated cost of all the facts deferred.

### 2.9 The Social Physics of Boardrooms

Boards operate as high-status micro-societies. Membership is earned through reputation, not experimentation. In such spaces, the **currency of belonging is getting along,** not curiosity.

Neuroscience confirms that dissent activates the same neural discomfort as physical pain.[2] The human brain trades accuracy for acceptance.

Hence, DT/DA endures not because people are corrupt but because the social physics reward conformity. Directors nod in rhythm, CEOs present polished decks, and everyone leaves believing they have fulfilled fiduciary duty. The ritual satisfies the *appearance* of oversight while starving its substance.

### 2.10 Incentives That Manufacture Silence

Compensation systems magnify the bias:

- **Short-term bonuses** link reward to calm optics rather than long-term resilience.
- **Board evaluation surveys** ask about "effectiveness of meetings," not truthfulness/relevance of information.
- **Audit ratings** measure compliance maturity, not decision relevance.

The outcome is a paradoxical economy where **predictable boredom and governance rituals are valued over unpredictable truth/reality**.

Executives who deliver "no issues to report" gain credibility; those who surface emerging uncertainty appear incompetent. Over time, honest reporting becomes career-limiting.

### 2.11 DT/DA as Emotional Regulation

Silence also serves a deeper psychological function: It regulates anxiety.

Complex systems generate uncertainty faster than humans can absorb it.[3] Boards subconsciously cap exposure by narrowing what they see.

This is why even catastrophic warning signs—boilerplate legal language, internal audit caveats—provoke no reaction; they exist below the board's emotional threshold.

PDG's contribution is to make uncertainty discussable without blame: when confidence, not control, becomes the metric, candour feels safe again.

### 2.12 Breaking the Cycle: Behaviour before Structure

Most governance reforms start with process: new reports, committees, more auditors, more risk specialists, and more governance rituals.[4] But

DT/DA is cured only when *behavioural norms* shift first. **Normalize Questioning.** Chairs must model curiosity—"What could make this objective fail?"

1. **Reframe Escalation.** Early warning becomes evidence of vigilance, not weakness.
2. **Protect the Messenger.** Institutionalize immunity for bad-news bearers.
3. **Reward Insight, Not Harmony.** Board evaluations should measure diversity of perspective.
4. **Visible Learning Loops.** When uncertainty drops because of early disclosure, celebrate it publicly.

These are micro-behaviours, but they recalibrate the entire climate of oversight.

### 2.13 From Syndrome to System: Transition to Chapter 3

DT/DA begins as human instinct but evolves into infrastructure: agendas that filter, dashboards that soothe, risk lists, highly edited internal audit reports, committees that partition.

Chapter 3—**The Cost of Purposeless Governance**—examines that structural evolution: How the behavioural silence of DT/DA becomes encoded in the very systems meant to inform boards.

*Culture writes the code; structure executes it.*

### Notes

1 This is a composite conclusion drawn from multiple sources. For a general discussion see www.mckinsey.com/featured-insights/mckinsey-explainers/what-is-psychological-safety

2 Separate neural representations for physical pain and social rejection, Choong-Wan Woo, Leonie Koban, Ethan Kross, Martin A. Lindquist, Marie T. Banich, Luka Ruzic, Jessica R. Andrews-Hanna, Tor D. Wager 2014, www.nature.com/articles/ncomms6380

3 This is a well-established conclusion across systems science, cybernetics, and behavioural economics rather than a single attributed quote.

4 For a high-level analysis of regulatory reform strategies post governance crisis over the past 50 years see Tim Leech/Lauren Hanlon article "Preventing

the next wave of unreliable financial reporting: Why US Congress should amend Section 404 of the Sarbanes – Oxley Act 2011 for a detailed analysis of regulatory response to multiple waves of massive/destructive governance failures". https://riskoversightsolutions.com/wp-content/uploads/2022/07/Open-Paper-LL-Why-US-Congress-Should-Amend-SO.pdf

# 3

# The Cost of Purposeless Governance

*When boards drift from purpose, economies drift with them and shareholders/broader stakeholders suffer.*

## 3.1 Introduction: Governance without Purpose Is Not Neutral; It Is Costly

Most directors assume that purpose is a philosophical consideration—important, but optional.

In reality, **the absence of purpose has measurable economic consequences**.

Evidence from multiple studies and authors over decades suggests that when organizational purpose is clear and embedded (not just stated), firms tend to show stronger subsequent performance; when trust/reputation is stronger, firms can benefit from a lower cost of equity. Research on organizational health also links stronger "operating systems" to more resilient performance through disruption.

Purposeless governance is not benign drift. It is a **structural deficiency that misallocates capital, distorts decision-making, and amplifies uncertainty**. This chapter examines *what that drift costs*—to companies, markets, societies, and the global economy.

## 3.2 Value Destruction: The Global Pattern

Every major corporate catastrophe of the last 50 years shares one root cause:

> Boards did not oversee the company's mission-critical objectives because the company had never defined them, and the board didn't think it was their job to oversee risk of achieving them.[1]

DOI: 10.1201/9781003685753-4 

This oversight vacuum produces **systematic value destruction,** visible in several categories:

#### *3.2.1 Market Capitalization Collapses*

Historical analysis of governance failures—from Enron to Boeing to Wirecard—shows multi-trillion-dollar market losses stemming from **purpose drift and oversight neglect.**

Boards focused on governance compliance rituals rather than the **top value-creation and value-preservation objectives** that truly determined survival.

#### *3.2.2 Strategic Execution Failures*

McKinsey's long-term studies show that 70% of strategic initiatives fail.[2]

The underlying cause is consistent:

**Boards review strategies, but not the associated mission-critical risks and uncertainties,** leaving them blind to execution barriers until failure is irreversible.

#### *3.2.3 Cost of Mispriced Risk*

Purposeless governance inflates risk in three ways:

1. **Underestimating strategic uncertainty** (e.g., ignoring current and emerging threats).
2. **Overestimating control strength** (trusting management's assurances and "green" dashboards without evidence).
3. **Misallocating resources** (spending heavily on compliance while underfunding MCO risk/uncertainty analysis and mitigation).

The economic effect is **systematic mispricing of risk,** contributing to volatility and lost opportunities.

### 3.3 Societal Costs: When Purpose Collapses, Trust Collapses

Organizations are social institutions. When their governance fails, societies absorb the consequences.

#### *3.3.1 Employment Shocks and Economic Cascades*

Corporate failures destroy more than equity—they wipe out livelihoods.

The collapse of a global manufacturer can disrupt **entire supply chains**, destabilizing local economies for years.

#### *3.3.2 Loss of Public Trust in Institutions*

Every scandal reduces confidence in boards, regulators, auditors, and capital markets.

Trust is the world's most undervalued economic asset—and the most expensive to lose.

#### *3.3.3 Reputational Contagion*

A high-profile governance failure in one company can tarnish entire sectors.

Banks, airlines, energy companies, and technology firms have experienced **reputational contagion effects** that depress valuations industry-wide.

### 3.4 The Financial Cost of "Checklist Governance"

Traditional governance frameworks encourage **ritual over relevance**:

- Strategic plans with little evidence key objectives being proposed were risk assessed.
- Risk registers disconnected from strategy and mission-critical objectives (MCOs) and performance.
- Audit plans and reports focused on management's internal control deficiencies.
- Committee agendas filled with boilerplate reports.
- Compliance reviews growing in volume, not value.

This "checklist governance" consumes vast resources including management and board time.

#### *3.4.1 The Cost of Redundant Assurance*

Global organizations routinely maintain:

- Enterprise Risk Management (ERM) groups
- Internal audit departments
- Compliance offices
- External auditors
- Growing number of specialized assurance units

Each produces independent reporting on **symptoms,** not on **MCOs.**

The result: **massive assurance spend without meaningful assurance.**

#### *3.4.2 The Accountability Mirage*

Boards receive increasing volumes of information, yet MCOs' oversight confidence remains low.

More reports create the illusion of control while obscuring what matters.

#### *3.4.3 The Opportunity Cost*

Thousands of hours invested in ritual assurance displace time and resources that should be spent on:

- Innovation
- Resilience planning
- Risk treatment optimization
- Talent development
- Bold strategic choices/moves
- Risk/uncertainty decisions
- Performance improvements

Purposeless governance is not simply ineffective—it is **expensive.**

### 3.5 The Quadrillion-Dollar Problem: Global Economic Drag

The cumulative cost of purposeless governance across the global economy is staggering.

Consider the impacts across five domains:

1. **Value Destruction from Preventable Failures**
   Corporate collapses, frauds, and crises cost **hundreds of billions annually** in lost equity and compensation.
2. **Misallocation of Capital**
   Without purpose as a guide, boards approve strategies that underperform and survive only through market momentum. The long-term drag on productivity is enormous.
3. **Regulatory Expansion**
   Every governance failure triggers new regulations, increasing compliance costs for all companies—even those that did nothing wrong (e.g. Sarbanes-Oxley section 404, FCPA (Foreign Corrupt Practices Act, Anti-Money Laundering), AML).
4. **Innovation Suppression**
   A governance environment obsessed with compliance produces risk-averse cultures, slowing innovation and economic dynamism.
5. **Trust Erosion across Capital Markets**
   Trust deficits translate into higher cost of capital and lower investor confidence.

A Deloitte analysis observed:
For example, one meta-analysis of the economic literature shows that a 10-percentage point increase in the share of trusting people within a country should raise annual per capita real GDP growth by about 0.5 percentage point. Economists estimate that **trust erosion reduces global GDP growth by up to 1% annually**.[3]

**Collectively, these factors amount to a multi-trillion-dollar drag on global economic performance—approaching the scale of a quadrillion-dollar long-term impact.**

### 3.6 The Human Consequences of Purposeless Leadership

Beyond economics, purposeless governance and purposeless boards harm people.

- Employees operate in uncertainty
- Whistleblowers are ignored

- Internal audit and risk staff feel irrelevant and not valued
- Customers and regulators lose faith
- Communities suffer when companies collapse

Purpose provides meaning.

Without it, organizations pursue **short-term, politically safe, low-value decisions** that betray the trust of the very stakeholders they exist to serve.

### 3.7 Purpose as the Missing Economic Control System

Boards cannot govern what they have not defined.
Without purpose:

- Objectives become vague
- Risk becomes abstract
- Reporting becomes ornamental
- Assurance becomes disconnected
- Oversight becomes reactive

Clear board purpose is the **root governance control**, and its absence is the **root cause of governance failure**. AI-supported research indicates only a very few boards globally define and disclose board purpose (less than 1%)[4]

A clear, disclosed, board-approved purpose functions as:

- **A strategic anchor**
- **A filter for capital allocation**
- **A map for identifying MCOs**
- **A lens for monitoring uncertainty**
- **A foundation for integrated assurance**

Purpose is not an idea.

It is an **economic system architecture**.

### 3.8 The Case for Purpose-Driven Governance (PDG)

This chapter sets the stage for what PDG solves:

1. **Purpose eliminates drift**
2. **MCOs eliminate blind spots**

3. **Confidence measures eliminate illusion**
4. **Integrated assurance eliminates duplication**
5. **Quantified uncertainty eliminates false comfort**

PDG is not a philosophical upgrade—it is a **performance upgrade**. It transforms governance from a cost centre into a **competitive advantage**.

### 3.9 Transition to Chapter 4: Mission-Critical Blindness

Chapter 4 explains how purposeless governance leads directly to the next systemic failure:

**The inability of boards to see, monitor, and govern core objectives that determine organizational survival.**

If Chapter 3 reveals the cost, Chapter 4 reveals the **mechanism** behind it.

### Notes

1 See Tim Leech article Board Oversight of Long-Term Value Creation and Preservation, Harvard Law School Forum on Corporate Governance, 2017 for an overview: https://corpgov.law.harvard.edu/2017/08/24/board-oversight-of-long-term-value-creation-and-preservation/

2 Common pitfalls in transformations: A conversation with Jon Garcia March 2022: www.mckinsey.com/capabilities/transformation/our-insights/common-pitfalls-in-transformations-a-conversation-with-jon-garcia?utm_source=chatgpt.com

3 The link between trust and economic prosperity: Repairing the global erosion of trust has economic advantages Deloitte, May 2021: www.deloitte.com/us/en/insights/topics/economy/connecting-trust-and-economic-growth.html?utm_source=chatgpt.com

4 Author to Chat GPT "What percentage of Canadian, US, and UK public companies disclose the board's PURPOSE?" Chat's response: "While exact figures are unavailable, based on available data and industry observations, it is estimated that fewer than 1% of public companies in these countries disclose a clear board purpose statement." www.linkedin.com/posts/tim-leech-01950013_most-agree-effective-boards-are-key-to-activity-7325127156781518849-tNoB/

# PART II

# THE CONSEQUENCES OF SILENCE

## When Governance Fails in Plain Sight

# 4
# Mission-Critical Blindness

*Governance collapses not because boards make bad decisions, but because they lack the information needed to oversee management's risk acceptance decisions on mission critical objectives key to sustained success.*

## 4.1 Introduction: The Blind Spot at the Heart of Oversight

If Chapter 3 exposed the Failure Information Loop inside organizations, Chapter 4 reveals its legal consequence:

**Boards have no reliable system to know whether their Mission-Critical Objective (MCOs) are on track or drifting towards failure.**

For decades, directors comforted themselves with dashboards, control attestations, and "top risks" lists—believing these artefacts constituted oversight. Delaware courts have now ended that illusion. Through a series of landmark "Caremark-plus" rulings, the judiciary has declared that **boards must ensure systems exist to detect, escalate, and act on red flags related to the enterprise's most vital objectives—not generic compliance categories.**

The modern interpretation of fiduciary duty has quietly shifted from *oversight of controls* to **oversight of the conditions that determine whether the organization will survive, comply, and perform.**

Most boards are not prepared for this shift.

DOI: 10.1201/9781003685753-6

## 4.2 The Evolution of Caremark: From Compliance to Mission-Critical Oversight

### *4.2.1 The Original 1996 Caremark Standard*

The original *In re Caremark International Inc. Derivative Litigation* decision set a minimal standard: Directors could be liable only if they utterly failed to implement a reporting system or intentionally ignored red flags.[1] For nearly two decades, this was viewed as an almost impossible bar to cross.

But the world changed—data scandals, product failures, misconduct, aircraft crashes, food safety disasters, opioid crises, cyber breaches. Courts began to ask:

**Were boards truly overseeing the company's most dangerous vulnerabilities?**

The answer, increasingly, was "no."

### *4.2.2* Marchand v. Barnhill (2019): *The Modern Trigger*

*Marchand*, triggered by a fatal listeria outbreak at Blue Bell Creameries, marked the turning point. The court held that food safety was the company's "mission-critical compliance risk"—and the board had no structured reporting system addressing it.[2]

Key message:

**Boards cannot rely on scattered operational updates. They require a formal system focused on the company's MCOs.**

### *4.2.3 Boeing, McDonald's, and the Rise of "Caremark-plus"*

Subsequent rulings pushed further:

- **Boeing (2019–2021):**[3] The board lacked systematic oversight of airplane safety, despite it being core to the company's existence.
- **McDonald's (2023):**[4] The court extended oversight failures to corporate culture and safety of the workforce.
- **Walgreens Boots Alliance,**[5] **AmerisourceBergen,**[6] **Wells Fargo:**[7] Boards were found plausibly unaware of risks directly tied to the company's legal, operational, or strategic viability.

Across multiple cases, one principle has solidified:

**Directors must know—reliably—whether MCOs are being achieved or endangered.**

**Failure to do so is now framed as a failure of good-faith oversight.**

This is the jurisprudential door through which Purpose-Driven Governance (PDG) walks naturally.

## 4.3 What Courts Now Expect: The Architecture of Good-Faith Oversight

Caremark today is no longer a compliance exercise—it is a legal expectation that boards must oversee **mission-critical risk and performance,** not just controls.

### *4.3.1 Expectation 1: Identify the Enterprise's MCOs*

Courts and powerful investors expect boards to explicitly understand what is truly mission-critical.

This is *not* a list of 200 risks. It is *not* the "top 10 enterprise risks."

It is the small set of objectives whose failure would:

- threaten solvency or viability;
- violate law or regulatory obligations;
- undermine trust or license to operate;
- destroy strategic value; and
- cause huge opportunities to create value to be overlooked.

For Boeing, it was "aircraft safety."

For Blue Bell, "food safety."

For financial institutions, "accuracy of financial reporting" and "liquidity integrity."

For healthcare, "patient safety."

For digital platforms, "data integrity and privacy."

Management and boards rarely articulate these explicitly. That is Mission-Critical Blindness.

#### *4.3.2 Expectation 2: Ensure Reliable Information Systems Exist*

Boards must ensure there are **structured, repeatable reporting systems** providing:

- identification of/agreement on MCOs;
- clear performance updates on MCOs;
- risk and uncertainty assessments linked to those objectives;
- early warning indicators; and
- assurance that risk/uncertainty status information reported to the board is reliable

Today's dashboards and risk registers do not meet this test.

#### *4.3.3 Expectation 3: Evidence of Active Engagement*

Courts, at least in the United States, now assess:

- Did the board ask the right questions?
- Was MCO risk information regularly reported to the board?
- Did the board act on red flags?
- Did minutes reflect actual oversight?

Silence is now evidence of failure.

#### *4.3.4 Expectation 4: A Closed-Loop Oversight System8*

Boards must demonstrate more than awareness—they must show:

1. **Mission-critical risk information reaching the board**
2. **Discussion and challenge**
3. **Direction and action**
4. **Follow-up and assurance**

This is the antithesis of the Don't Tell/Don't Ask Syndrome.
This is PDG in practice.

### 4.4 Why Mission-Critical Blindness Is So Common

#### *4.4.1 Mistaking Fragmented Reporting for Oversight*

Boards confuse volume with visibility.

The reality: the more fragmented the reporting, the more likely mission-critical issues are invisible.

#### *4.4.2 Risk Registers That Don't Link to Objectives*

Nearly all risk programs operate on "risk lists," not linked to top value-creation and value-preservation objectives. The company's MCOs.

Courts, particularly Chancery Court in Delaware, now view this as inadequate.

#### *4.4.3 Internal Audit and Risk Functions Operating in Compliance Mode*

Most internal audit and risk groups still focus on individual disparate risks divorced from objectives and performance, controls, policies, and compliance findings—not on the entity's MCOs.

Thus, boards receive audits of symptoms, not causes; controls, not objectives.

#### *4.4.4 Cultural Convenience: The Don't Tell/Don't Ask Loop*

Mission-Critical Blindness is comfortable—until it's catastrophic.

Executives avoid disclosing uncertainty; boards avoid demanding clarity.

This mutual avoidance is now a legal liability, not just a cultural flaw.

### 4.5 Lessons from Recent Cases: How Boards Can Lose the Protection of the Business Judgment Rule

The business judgment rule in most countries protects directors who make informed decisions in good faith.

But courts are signalling in multiple cases that **this protection evaporates** when boards:

- cannot show structured oversight of MCOs'
- rely on ad hoc reporting;
- fail to respond to repeated red flags;
- lack evidence of discussion and follow-up; and
- delegate oversight without ensuring systems exist.

Boards do not need to guarantee outcomes.

But they must demonstrate **a system capable of detecting and responding to significant threats to mission-critical outcomes.**

This is a subtle but transformative shift.

### 4.6 Mission-Critical Blindness: The Measurable Cost

The consequences of this blindness are massive:

- multi-trillion-dollar regulatory and D&O insurance settlements[9]
- executive turnover and reputational damage
- regulator intervention
- shareholder derivative claims
- class actions and D&O coverage disputes
- destroyed trust, delayed strategy execution, lost competitiveness

Behind almost every crisis lies the same pattern:

**The board did not have reliable information on the risk/uncertainty status of the company's most vital objectives—MCOs.**

### 4.7 The PDG View: What Boards Must Do Now

This book argues that courts are articulating—implicitly—the foundation of PDG. Boards must:

1. **define and disclose their purpose;**
2. **call on management to identify MCOs that give effect to that purpose;**
3. **ensure structured oversight systems exist for each MCO;**
4. **demand risk and assurance reporting linked directly to each MCO;**
5. **break the Don't Tell/Don't Ask culture; and**
6. **require independent assurance on the reliability of MCO risk/uncertainty status information.**

Caremark jurisprudence is not a threat—it is a roadmap.

A roadmap towards PDG and Mission-Critical Oversight becoming the global standard.

### 4.8 Conclusion: The End of Plausible Deniability

Boards can no longer hide behind the comfortable fiction of "we were not told."

Modern fiduciary duty is clear:

**Directors must create the conditions to be told—truthfully, consistently, and early—about risk/uncertainty linked to MCOs.**

Mission-Critical Blindness is neither accidental nor inevitable.

It is the product of governance systems designed around compliance, not purpose.

PDG provides the architecture to correct this.

The question now is simple—and central to the Quadrillion-Dollar Question:

**Will boards rebuild their oversight systems around MCOs, or wait for courts and crises to force them?**

#### Notes

1 Boards Duty of Care: Continuing Travails from Caremark to Boeing, Joseph P Monteleone and H Stephen Grace, May 2024: www.americanbar.org/groups/business_law/resources/business-law-today/2024-may/boards-duty-oversight-caremark-continuing-travails-boeing/?utm_source=chatgpt.com
2 A Director's Duty of Oversight after Marchand in "Caremark" Case, Harvard Law School Forum on Corporate Governance, Jan 2022: https://corpgov.law.harvard.edu/2022/01/23/a-directors-duty-of-oversight-after-marchand-in-caremark-case/?utm_source=chatgpt.com
3 Boeing 737 Max investigation, House Committee on Transportation and Infrastructure, 2017–2020: https://democrats-transportation.house.gov/committee-activity/boeing-737-max-investigation
4 Recapping the McDonald's Delaware court decision – Duty of oversight and D&O considerations, Andrew Moss, Jalen Brown, 2023: www.reedsmith.com/our-insights/blogs/the-policyholder-perspective/102k340/recapping-the-mcdonalds-delaware-court-decision-duty-of-oversight-and-do-cons/?utm_source=chatgpt.com
5 Walgreens Boots Alliance's board of directors has faced multiple accusations of **negligence** in various legal actions, including shareholder lawsuits related to the opioid crisis, the failed Rite Aid merger, and recent poor financial performance.
6 Stockholder derivative lawsuits have alleged that the AmerisourceBergen (now Cencora) board of directors was negligent in its oversight duties,

particularly regarding illegal drug distribution programs and the opioid crisis.

7 Wells Fargo's board of directors faced significant accusations and findings of negligence for failing to provide adequate oversight, allowing systemic sales misconduct (like creating fake accounts) to flourish despite internal warnings, and not establishing proper controls, leading to major fines, executive firings, and personal penalties for directors for breach of fiduciary duty and oversight failures.

8 Author note: Country-specific legal advice on board's fiduciary duty of care/oversight strongly recommended to determine country specific director fiduciary duty of care.

9 For more details see "Mission Critical": Director Liability Ticking Time Bomb, Tim Leech, The D&O Diary, December 2024: www.dandodiary.com/2024/12/articles/corporate-governance/guest-post-mission-critical-director-liability-ticking-time-bomb/

# 5
# The Failure Information Loop

*When the right information fails to flow, oversight becomes governance theatre.*

## 5.1 Introduction: The Invisible Architecture of Oversight Failure

Every major governance scandal of the last four decades shares a common defect:

**Boards, the people charged with management oversight and making the most consequential decisions, often receive the least reliable information.**[1]

This chapter examines the structural root cause of that gap.

It is not incompetence. It is not malice. It is not lack of data.

It is **information asymmetry**—a widening disconnect between:

- what **management** knows (or could/should know);
- what **boards** actually see; and
- what **shareholders** assume the board is seeing.

The result is a self-reinforcing failure cycle: **The Failure Information Loop,** a loop so embedded in modern organizations that directors do not even perceive it operating.

## 5.2 The Three Layers of Asymmetry

### *5.2.1 Layer 1: Management's Knowledge—High Volume, Low Integration*

Within the organization, information is abundant but fragmented.

Management teams generate hundreds of reports, KPIs, risk lists, audit findings, and operational dashboards.

DOI: 10.1201/9781003685753-7

Yet almost none of this information is tied to risk linked to **Mission-Critical Objectives (MCOs).**

Executives operate inside voluminous data but poor synthesis.

This produces an illusion of control:

"We have lots of information, therefore we must be well informed."

The opposite is often true.

#### *5.2.2 Layer 2: Board Information—Low Volume, High Filtering*

Boards receive a small, polished, selectively filtered subset of the above. Information flows through:

- the CEO's discretion
- management's interpretation of what directors "need to know"
- dashboards designed to reassure rather than to reveal risk
- risk heat maps sanitized of mission-critical uncertainty
- audit reports often focused on relatively minor control exceptions, not existential objectives

Directors cannot absorb the underlying complexity because they are never shown it.

#### *5.2.3 Layer 3: Shareholders' Assumptions—High Trust, Low Verification*

Investors assume that boards have systems to know:

- whether strategy is on track;
- whether MCOs are being achieved;
- whether risk linked to MCOs is rising or falling; and
- whether disclosures are reliable.

They assume boards are receiving real relevant information.

At most companies, they are not.

This assumption gap—between what shareholders imagine and what boards actually know—is now a governance liability with measurable economic consequences.

### 5.3 The Failure Information Loop Explained

The Failure Information Loop operates through four reinforcing steps:

### *5.3.1 Step 1: Fragmented Generation*

Operations generate huge quantities of data, but little of it is tied to risk/uncertainty linked to MCOs—top strategic/value-creation and value-preservation objectives.

No single system shows:

**Are our MCOs at risk or on track?**

### *5.3.2 Step 2: Distorted Aggregation*

Middle and senior managers aggregate information to "tell the story" they believe the board expects.

This introduces optimism bias, political filtering, and omission of uncertainty.

In many companies only "green" and occasional "yellow" metrics survive the climb upward.

### *5.3.3 Step 3: Sanitized Presentation*

Boards receive curated summaries—heat maps, risk lists, compliance statistics, and internal audit reports with what IA (Internal Audit) sees as management's internal control deficiencies.

Missing entirely is the only question courts and shareholders increasingly care about:

**What is the current level of risk and uncertainty linked to each MCO?**

### *5.3.4 Step 4: False Feedback*

Boards, believing they have been well-informed, offer direction based on incomplete or inaccurate information.

Management interprets this as validation.

The system loops:

**Management filters → Boards assume clarity → Shareholders assume oversight → Reality drifts.**

This loop can continue for years until a crisis forces the truth into daylight—by which time value has already been destroyed.

## 5.4 Why Traditional Enterprise Risk Management (ERM) Cannot Fix the Loop

Traditional ERM—rooted in risk registers, heat maps, and lists of hazards/bad things that could happen—is structurally incapable of repairing the Failure Information Loop.

### *5.4.1 ERM Tracks Risks, Not Objectives*

ERM catalogues risks as isolated items, not as uncertainties affecting specific MCOs.

Thus, boards never see the full picture of how risk affects/could affect performance on key objectives.

### *5.4.2 ERM Prioritizes Discrete Events, Not Integrated Outcomes*

Risk registers fragment reality into boxes. But crises emerge from interactions across objectives—something risk registers cannot model.

### *5.4.3 ERM Rewards Reporting, Not Understanding*

Risk owners produce narratives to satisfy the framework, not insight to support decision-making.

The exercise becomes bureaucratic, not strategic.

### *5.4.4 ERM Lives below the Board Line*

Boards almost never see MCO-centric risk/uncertainty assessments.

They see stylized outputs that obscure uncertainty rather than illuminate it.

Traditional ERM was built to support internal control and regulatory compliance—not demand-driven board oversight of MCOs and performance.

It cannot fix the Failure Information Loop because **it was never designed to.**

## 5.5 Why Traditional Internal Audit Cannot Fix the Loop

Traditional IA is also structurally misaligned.

#### *5.5.1 IA Focuses on Controls, Not Objectives*

Boards receive pages of what internal audit sees as management's internal control "deficiencies and weaknesses." Little of what most internal audit units do today provides direct insight re risk/uncertainty linked to the enterprise's MCOs.

Thus, audit results rarely shift strategic decision-making.

#### *5.5.2 IA Provides Rear-View Assurance*

Audits look backward.

MCO oversight requires forward-looking insight.

#### *5.5.3 IA Reports at the Wrong Level of Materiality*

Directors need assurance on existential objectives—reliability of disclosures, safety, liquidity, culture, product quality, top strategic/value creation objectives.

IA reports on topics it is allowed to cover like purchase requisitions/ orders, accounts payable, financial accounting processes, policy breaches, and minor exceptions. Few internal audit units report on composite risk/uncertainty to MCOs—likelihood key objectives will be achieved with a level of risk/uncertainty acceptable to CEO and board.

#### *5.5.4 IA Reinforces Filtering Behaviour*

Management often negotiates audit findings, further sanitizing what reaches the board.

Traditional IA cannot fix the loop because **it also operates inside it.**

### 5.6 Why the Loop Persists: The Governance-Incentive Problem

Three forces sustain the Failure Information Loop:

1. **Political Incentives**
   Executives are rewarded for good news.
   Bad news—especially about MCOs—creates personal risk.

2. **Cognitive Comfort**
   Boards prefer clarity, even if false, to complexity that exposes fragility.
   Risk and control theatre feels better than oversight reality.
3. **Structural Blindness (Don't Tell/Don't Ask Governance Syndrome)**

   Management avoids telling; boards avoid asking.
   Both sides declare victory in the illusion of alignment.
   The loop is not accidental.
   It is systemic.

### 5.7 Breaking the Loop Requires a New Oversight Architecture

Purpose-Driven Governance and Mission-Critical ERM/IA were designed precisely to break this loop.

Boards must demand systems that:

- define MCOs;
- link risks, risk treatments, performance, and uncertainty to each MCO;
- escalate red flags automatically;
- provide directors with reliable, unfiltered insight;
- include independent assurance on MCO risk/uncertainty status reliability
- close the loop with documented board deliberation and follow-up

Only an **objective-centric, purpose-anchored, closed-loop** governance system can restore information symmetry.

### 5.8 Conclusion: Until the Loop Breaks, Oversight Is an Illusion

The Failure Information Loop is the quiet engine behind most governance failures.

It keeps boards confident but uninformed.
It keeps management busy but not transparent.
It keeps shareholders trusting but vulnerable.
Traditional ERM cannot fix it.

Traditional IA cannot fix it.

Only a governance system built around **purpose, MCOs,** and **transparent MCOs risk/uncertainty reporting** can restore oversight integrity.

The loop is powerful.

But it is not inevitable.

Companies and boards can break it—once they choose to see it.

## Note

1 For an overview of multiple waves of governance failures since 1970s see Preventing the next wave of unreliable financial reporting: Why US Congress should amend Section 404 of the Sarbanes – Oxley Act, Tim Leech, Lauren Leech July 2011, *International Journal of Governance and Disclosure*: https://riskoversightsolutions.com/wp-content/uploads/2022/07/Open-Paper-LL-Why-US-Congress-Should-Amend-SO.pdf

# 6
# When Culture Becomes a Control Failure

*Culture doesn't eat strategy for breakfast. It eats effective Mission Critical Objectives' risk management and oversight.*

### 6.1 Introduction: The Myth of Cultural Comfort

Boards love to talk about "tone at the top"—the idea that values flow downward from leadership, shaping behaviour, and setting ethical guardrails. But tone at the top is not a control. It is a **belief**. And belief, without evidence, is aspiration masquerading as assurance.

In reality, culture is often the largest unmonitored risk in an organization.[1]

It determines:

- what gets escalated;
- what gets suppressed;
- what behaviours are rewarded;
- what truths are politically dangerous; and
- what information flows up—and what dies in the middle.

This chapter shows how **denial, groupthink, and incentive design** transform culture into an active control failure, even in companies with what are touted as world-class ERM frameworks, huge internal audit functions, sophisticated dashboards, and experienced boards.

Three cases—Wells Fargo, Boeing, and Wirecard—illustrate this truth: **Where culture contradicts governance, culture wins.**

### 6.2 Culture as a Governance System: The Unseen Architecture

Culture is not a "soft" concept. It is a parallel governance system operating underneath formal structures and processes.

 DOI: 10.1201/9781003685753-8

It determines:

- **how risk is perceived;**
- **what is considered acceptable uncertainty;**
- **who feels safe telling the truth;**
- **which Mission-Critical Objectives (MCOs) are silently deprioritized; and**
- **how leadership reacts to red flags.**

Most importantly, an entity's culture dictates whether Mission-Critical Blindness and the Failure Information Loop are reinforced—or broken.

In many companies, culture acts as an invisible algorithm governing behaviour:

**If telling the truth carries more personal risk than staying silent, silence becomes the dominant behaviour.**

This is the Don't Ask/Don't Tell Governance Syndrome in its purest form.

### 6.3 Case Study 1: Wells Fargo[2]—Incentives That Overpowered Integrity

#### *6.3.1 The MCO Misalignment*

Wells Fargo's MCOs included customer trust, ethical sales conduct, and regulatory compliance. Yet its internal incentive structures tied compensation to aggressive cross-selling metrics. The board saw rising sales numbers—**not** the underlying pressure that was driving fraudulent accounts.

#### *6.3.2 Red Flags That Never Reached the Board*

Years of whistleblower complaints, internal ethics hotline reports, and audit findings were filtered or reframed as isolated issues. The Failure Information Loop was fully active: management assured the board that cultural issues were "being addressed," when in fact they were systemic.

#### *6.3.3 Culture Overpowered Controls*

The company's stated values could not overcome:

- fear of retaliation
- performance-driven distortion
- a culture that celebrated numbers, not truth

The board trusted tone at the top; regulators later documented a **systemic cultural control failure**.

The lesson:

**When incentives reward misconduct, culture becomes the root cause of risk—not just a contributor to it.**

### 6.4 Case Study 2: Boeing—Denial as a Cultural Operating Model[3]

#### *6.4.1 MCO: Safety above All*

For Boeing, aircraft safety is existential—its ultimate MCO. Yet cultural deterioration after the McDonnell Douglas merger shifted priorities towards schedule and shareholder returns, subtly undermining engineering integrity.

#### *6.4.2 Pressure, Fear, and Information Distortion*

Engineers repeatedly signalled concerns about Mission Critical Aircraft Safety (MCAS) and the pressures to meet 737 MAX deadlines. But cultural norms discouraged escalation. Warnings were "managed," not amplified.

Boeing's board received:

- compliance reports
- manufacturing updates
- safety briefings

But not the truth: that core safety assumptions had been compromised.

#### *6.4.3 The Board's Cultural Blind Spot*

Boeing's board had extraordinary technical competence but relied heavily on management narratives. There was no structured system requiring **independent, objective, MCO-aligned safety reporting**.

Tone at the top was strong; truth at the bottom was suppressed.

The lesson:

**When culture prioritizes speed and optics, mission-critical safety oversight becomes impossible—even for experienced directors.**

## 6.5 Case Study 3: Wirecard[4]—Groupthink and the Illusion of Genius

### *6.5.1 MCO: Trust in Financial Reporting*

For a high-growth fintech, trust in financial disclosures is mission-critical. Yet Wirecard's culture idolized its CEO and CFO, framing sceptics as enemies and short-sellers as bad actors.

### *6.5.2 A Culture Designed to Block Scrutiny*

Red flags were plentiful: investigative journalism, regulatory warnings, external audit concerns, whistleblowers. But groupthink—built on arrogance and loyalty—overpowered institutional curiosity.

Information to the board was filtered through a charismatic management team whose confidence masked the absence of evidence.

### *6.5.3 Governance Theatre*

The board believed it had strong controls:

- ERM frameworks
- internal audit
- compliance structures
- annual external audits

But these were façades.

When culture is built on intimidation and myth-making, controls become ornamental.

The lesson:

**Groupthink can render any oversight system useless.**

## 6.6 The Common Cultural Failure Pattern

Across these cases, three cultural forces emerge as consistent drivers of governance collapse.

#### *6.6.1 Denial: When Hope Replaces Evidence*

Leadership resists acknowledging risks, fearing reputational damage or personal accountability.

Denial creates a cognitive shield that blocks escalation of bad news.

#### *6.6.2 Groupthink: When Dissent Is Socially Unsafe*

Homogeneous thinking eliminates challenge. Directors nod in alignment, mistaking harmony for clarity.

Dissenters self-censor because challenging the group becomes a threat, not a duty.

#### *6.6.3 Incentives: When Rewards Encourage Misconduct*

Pay structures reward the wrong behaviours: sales over ethics, speed over safety, loyalty over truth.

Compensation plans become cultural accelerators—and cultural accelerants.

These forces reinforce the Don't Ask/Don't Tell Governance Syndrome and amplify the Failure Information Loop.

### 6.7 Why Traditional Tools Cannot Detect or Challenge Cultural Failure

#### *6.7.1 Tone at the Top Is Not Evidence*

Boards consistently overestimate cultural health because senior leaders confidently assure them "our culture is strong" or they prefer not knowing.

Without verification, this becomes governance vulnerability.

#### *6.7.2 ERM Does Not Measure Cultural Risk*

Risk registers do not capture:

- fear of speaking up
- the reliability of escalation channels
- incentive misalignment
- political filtering

Hence, risk list ERM frequently reports cultural stability when cultural fragility is rising.

#### *6.7.3 Internal Audit Is Often Culturally Constrained*

IA teams are frequently pressured to "stay in their lane," focusing on policies, controls, compliance and relatively small exceptions—not the cultural conditions and risks undermining MCOs. Few assess/report to boards on risk/uncertainty linked to MCOs. They aren't trained to, or allowed to, at most companies today.

Auditors rarely report the truth about culture because doing so is often politically dangerous.

### 6.8 Culture as a Board Oversight Obligation

Modern fiduciary duty—amplified by Caremark and its progeny—via regulatory expectations now requires boards to oversee cultural risks as seriously as financial risks.

Boards must be able to answer:

- **Is our culture enabling or suppressing truth?**
- **Do people feel safe escalating concerns?**
- **Do incentives align with our MCOs?**
- **What evidence—not management assurances—proves this?**

Boards cannot rely on management's self-assessment claims.

They need:

- independent cultural diagnostics
- employee voice systems
- whistleblower trend analysis
- objective reporting on MCO-linked risk disclosures and behaviours
- assurance that cultural indicators are reliable

This is Purpose-Driven Governance applied to culture.

### 6.9 Breaking the Cultural Control Failure

Boards that wish to prevent Wells Fargo, Boeing, or Wirecard-style failures and the like must:

1. **define cultural expectations tied directly to MCOs;**
2. **require systematic upward reporting on cultural indicators;**
3. **ensure executive incentives reinforce—not distort—desired behaviour;**
4. **provide safe channels for truth-telling;**
5. **demand independent assurance on cultural health; and**
6. **document board discussions and follow-up on cultural red flags.**

Without these, culture becomes the single greatest source of oversight risk.

### 6.10 Conclusion: Culture Is Not "Soft"; It Is Structural

Culture is not what companies say.

Culture is what people feel safe doing and saying.

In Wells Fargo, employees feared honesty.

In Boeing, engineers feared delay.

In Wirecard, truth itself became a threat.

In every case, culture became a massive **control failure**—one powerful enough to override policies, governance frameworks, and board expertise.

Until boards treat culture as a measurable, mission-critical system rather than a feel-good narrative, Don't Tell/Don't Ask Governance Syndrome will continue to thrive.[5]

The next chapter will show how the Missing Purpose, Mission-Critical Blindness, the Failure Information Loop, and Cultural Control Failure converge—creating the perfect conditions for governance collapse, and the roadmap required to prevent it.

### Notes

1 For a more rigorous discussion of board oversight of culture see "The Next Frontier for Boards, Oversight of Risk Culture," Professor Parveen Gupta, Tim Leech, Harvard Law Forum on Corporate Governance, July 2015: https://corpgov.law.harvard.edu/2015/07/13/the-next-frontier-for-boards-oversight-of-risk-culture

2 For details on OCC findings re Wells Fargo governance failure the written opinions of the administrative judge that heard the OCC cases against Wells

Fargo officers, including CEO, CLO, CRO and two CAEs are available at: www.occ.gov/topics/laws-and-regulations/enforcement-actions/comptrollers-orders.html. Some are as long as 300 pages (search for Wells Fargo).

3 Delaware Chancery Court decision allowing a derivative shareholder action against the Boeing directors to proceed is available at: https://courts.delaware.gov/Opinions/Download.aspx?id=324120. The court decided to allow the action against directors to proceed. The case was settled out of court, but there were numerous other regulatory actions and hearings on what went wrong at Boeing that are too numerous to list resulting in billions of dollars of fines/settlements.

4 A high-level overview of the Wirecard governance failure is available at: https://en.wikipedia.org/wiki/Wirecard_scandal. It has scores of links to specific inquiries and investigations launched.

5 Readers are encouraged to access and read the corporate culture diagnostic tool Tim Leech developed to measure corporate culture. It is available free at: https://riskoversightsolutions.com/wp-content/uploads/2020/12/Risk-Oversight-Solutions-Risk-Culture-Survey-for-Objective-Centric-ERM-IA.pdf It has clear linkages to many of the points made in this chapter. Low culture scores should be seen as high risk that board is not receiving reliable information on risk/uncertainty linked to MCOs.

# PART III

# THE ARCHITECTURE OF PURPOSE

## Designing Governance That Works

# 7

# Re-Engineering Governance for the 21st Century

*Governance doesn't need another checklist. It needs a new architecture.*

## 7.1 Introduction: Why Legacy Governance Can't Be Fixed with Tweaks

Chapters 1–6 diagnose the problem; Chapter 7 begins the cure.

The central insight is simple but radical:

**Modern governance is structurally incapable of doing what society now demands of boards and companies.**

Incremental fixes—better dashboards, more board education, new ESG (Environment, Social, Governance) rules, more board committees, expanded risk registers—cannot solve systemic design flaws.

The 21st century requires a new governance architecture that:

- begins with clear board **purpose;**
- focuses oversight on **Mission-Critical Objectives (MCOs);**
- integrates risk and uncertainty into **decision-making;**
- restores information symmetry between management and the board; and
- includes **assurance** on the reliability of what boards are told.

That architecture is **Purpose-Driven Governance (PDG).**

DOI: 10.1201/9781003685753-10

## 7.2 Why Governance Must Shift from Checklists to Objectives

### *7.2.1 The Checklist Era Is Over*

For decades, governance evolved by adding more requirements:

- more independence
- more committees
- more policies
- more compliance
- more auditors and risk specialists
- more disclosures
- more risk lists and audit reports on what internal audit sees as management's "internal control deficiencies"

Boards became experts in reviewing inputs—but blind to whether the most vital outcomes were being achieved.

### *7.2.2 Boards Need Insight, Not Artefacts*

The real oversight questions are outcome-based:

- Are we achieving our MCOs?
- What uncertainties threaten them?
- What opportunities are there we aren't exploiting?
- What is being done to treat/address those uncertainties?
- What is the state of our culture, safety, and ethical guardrails?
- Is disclosure information reliable?
- Are we protecting existence and enabling performance?

Traditional governance does not organize itself around these questions. PDG does.

## 7.3 PDG: The Foundational Shift

PDG begins with a simple truth:

**Boards exist to ensure the organization's purpose is fulfilled.**

Every element of oversight—risk, audit, strategy, incentives, assurance—must align to that purpose.

PDG introduces three structural shifts:

1. **Purpose replaces compliance as the anchor of governance.**
2. **MCOs risk/uncertainty status reports replace risk lists and internal control deficiency reports as the focus of oversight.**
3. **Integrated uncertainty and assurance replace fragmented reporting and trust-based oversight.**

This is governance re-engineered—from first principles.

## 7.4 The Four Pillars of PDG

PDG rests on four mutually reinforcing pillars that create a closed-loop oversight system.

### *7.4.1 Pillar 1: Purpose Clarification and Disclosure*

Boards must define and publicly disclose their purpose—not just the organization's purpose/mission, but the **board's purpose**:

- Why does this board exist?
- What outcomes is it accountable for ensuring?
- What principles govern its decisions?
- Does the board see overseeing risk linked to MCOs as part of the board's purpose?

This is the missing foundation in nearly every global framework—from Delaware law to the UK Code to COSO/NACD's most recent effort to develop corporate governance guidance, guidance that was unexpectedly aborted in July 2025 with no explanation after being issued for public comment in May.

Without clarity of board purpose, oversight becomes reactive, fragmented, and ultimately symbolic.

PDG makes purpose the governance anchor.

### *7.4.2 Pillar 2: Identification of MCOs*

Purpose becomes operational only when management and the board agree the small set of objectives whose failure would threaten the organization's viability, trust, strategy, or license to operate.

These include:

- Value-preservation objectives (e.g., safety, reliable reporting, liquidity, compliance integrity)
- Strategic/value-creation objectives (e.g., strategic initiatives, major transformations, critical growth drivers)

MCOs give directors a clear, focused oversight agenda—replacing the hundreds of unprioritized risks and metrics that overwhelm boards today.

#### *7.4.3 Pillar 3: Objective-Centric Oversight of Risk and Uncertainty*

PDG aligns risk/uncertainty assessment directly to each MCO.

The board no longer asks:

"What are the top risks?"

It asks:

**"What uncertainties could prevent us from achieving each Mission-Critical Objective?"**

**"How severe could the impact be?"**

**"How reliable is the information on risk/uncertainty status we are receiving?"**

This shift transforms risk from a compliance exercise into a strategic discipline.

Boards gain insight into:

- expected and actual performance
- positive and negative uncertainty
- early warning indicators
- emerging threats
- management's risk acceptance decisions
- confidence levels in management reporting

This is the oversight that Caremark, investors, and society increasingly require.

#### *7.4.4 Pillar 4: Integrated Assurance—Evidence, Not Optimism*

PDG does not rely on trust or tone at the top.

It requires **independent assurance** linked to each MCO on:

- reliability and adequacy of performance reporting
- reliability of risk/uncertainty status reports provided to the board
- reliability of culture and behavioural indicators
- existence and adequacy of risk treatments/controls related to mission-critical outcomes

Internal audit's paradigm shifts from control policing to **assurance on mission-critical truth.**

This closes the Failure Information Loop and breaks Don't Tell / Don't Ask.

## 7.5 The PDG Operating Rhythm: A Closed-Loop Oversight System

PDG structures governance into a repeatable operating cycle:

1. **Define board purpose, including MCO oversight**
2. **Define entity purpose and MCOs**
3. **Assess uncertainty to each MCO**
4. **Report MCO status to the board—integrated performance, uncertainty, culture, early warnings**
5. **Board challenges, sets direction, ensures risk response**
6. **Independent assurance verifies reliability of information**
7. **Board follows up and adapts strategy and oversight**

This creates a governance system capable of continuous learning and early detection of failure conditions—something legacy governance cannot do.

## 7.6 Why PDG Resolves the Structural Failures of Modern Governance

### *7.6.1 It Eliminates Mission-Critical Blindness*

Boards now know exactly which objectives matter most and have reliable information on their uncertainty/risk status.

#### *7.6.2 It Breaks the Failure Information Loop*

Filtering is replaced with structured, objective-centric reporting, and independent verification.

#### *7.6.3 It Overcomes Cultural Control Failures*

Assurance on culture, incentives, and behavioural indicators ensures truth rises to the board.

#### *7.6.4 It Rebalances Power between Board and Management*

Boards no longer depend on selectively curated narratives.

They receive structured evidence tied to entity purpose and MCOs.

#### *7.6.5 It Aligns Governance with Modern Legal Expectations*

Delaware's Caremark-plus cases effectively describe PDG's requirements—without offering the blueprint.

PDG provides that blueprint.

### 7.7 What the 21st Century Demands—A Governance Model Built for Uncertainty

The world facing boards today is defined by:

- exponential technological risk
- geopolitical uncertainty
- reputational fragility
- climate and sustainability pressures
- massive regulatory expectations
- cultural complexity
- shareholder activism
- AI-enabled disruption and risk

Legacy governance, designed for a slower, more stable era, cannot cope.

PDG is designed for:

- high uncertainty
- rapid complexity
- mission-critical accountability
- real-time information demands
- multi-stakeholder trust expectations
- optimal use of AI capabilities

Boards that adopt PDG gain a structural advantage:

**They can see reality sooner.**
**They can act faster.**
**They can prevent value destruction instead of explaining it.**

### 7.8 Conclusion: Governance Must Be Rebuilt, Not Refreshed/Tweaked

Governance reform movements around the world offer incremental improvements—longer and more governance codes, new reporting rules, updated guidelines. But the problems revealed in Chapters 1–6 are architectural, not procedural.

**You can't fix a broken house with new curtains.**

**You need a new foundation.**

**Or, as my grandfather a hunting/fishing guide would say more bluntly, you can't put lipstick on a pig.**

PDG is that foundation.

It re-centres boards on their true role:

**ensuring that entity purpose is achieved, mission-critical outcomes are realized, uncertainty is understood, and the truth reaches the boardroom.**

In the chapters that follow, PDG moves from architectural model to implementation roadmap—showing boards, executives, risk leaders, and auditors how to operationalize a 21st-century governance system capable of delivering trust, resilience, performance, and transparency.

# 8

# From Diagnosis to Design

## The Strategic Blueprint

*Diagnosis reveals what's broken. Design reveals what's possible.*

### 8.1 Introduction: Turning Insight into Architecture

The preceding chapters identified a pattern of structural governance failures:

- **The Purpose Void** (Chapter 1)
- **Don't Tell/Don't Ask Governance Syndrome** (Chapter 2)
- **Mission-Critical Blindness** (Chapter 4)
- **The Failure Information Loop** (Chapter 5)
- **Cultural Control Failure** (Chapter 6)

Together these failures form what this book names **the Quadrillion-Dollar Problem** quantified in Chapter 3—the global, systemic destruction of value and missed opportunities in companies where boards operate without reliable information on the risk status of Mission-Critical Objectives (MCOs). The vast knowledge, experiences, and expertise of boards are not being optimized by the companies they oversee.

Diagnosis alone is not enough.

Boards need a **design blueprint**—a practical, repeatable, engineering-grade architecture that prevents these failures and aligns purpose, performance, risk, and reward.

That blueprint is **Purpose-Driven Governance (PDG)**, supported operationally by **Objective-Centric Risk & Uncertainty Management (OCRUM)**.

This chapter explains how the two integrate to form a complete oversight system.


DOI: 10.1201/9781003685753-11

## 8.2 Why Governance Needs Engineering, Not Incremental Reform

Traditional governance is built on interpretations, codes, and professional norms.

It is not engineered. It evolved—piecemeal, reactive, siloed.

Engineering disciplines start from design principles, not tradition. They ask:

- What is the system supposed to achieve?
- What are the critical failure points?
- What inputs, processes, and controls ensure the desired outcome?
- What feedback loops provide reliability?

Governance must now be treated with the same rigour as aviation, nuclear safety, cybersecurity, and financial system design.

PDG is the first governance approach that applies engineering logic to the oversight of corporate purpose and mission-critical performance.

## 8.3 The Strategic Blueprint: Seven Design Principles of PDG

The PDG–OCRUM blueprint rests on seven scientific design principles. Each corrects one or more structural deficiencies diagnosed earlier.

### *8.3.1 Principle 1: Purpose Is the System Anchor*

Every engineered system begins with a defined purpose.

In governance, this means:

- articulate the organization's purpose and MCOs;
- define the board's purpose, including MCO oversight; and
- align structures, internal audit and risk, and information flows to those purposes.

Without purpose clarity, oversight becomes arbitrary.

With clarity, oversight becomes directional, measurable, and strategic.

*8.3.2 Principle 2: MCOs Are the Oversight Core*

Purpose becomes operational through a small set of MCOs—the outcomes that matter most for survival, performance, value creation, trust, and compliance.

Identifying MCOs allows boards to:

- prioritize
- focus oversight
- concentrate resources
- understand uncertainty
- oversee management's risk taking
- demand evidence

This single step eliminates Mission-Critical Blindness and frames the entire oversight agenda.

*8.3.3 Principle 3: Uncertainty Is a Performance Variable*

OCRUM treats uncertainty as a collection of threats to achievement and opportunities to MCOs key performance.

Management and boards must see:

- upside uncertainty (opportunities)
- downside uncertainty (risks/threats to achievement)
- emerging patterns
- velocity, exposure, and interdependence

This transforms risk management from a compliance ritual into a strategic forecasting and decision support/performance improvement discipline.

*8.3.4 Principle 4: Decision-Useful Information Must Flow Upward*

The Failure Information Loop thrives when truth is filtered.

PDG requires structured, repeatable reporting systems that provide:

- MCO performance status
- linked uncertainty/risk assessments
- early warning indicators

- cultural and behavioural metrics
- management's confidence levels targets will be achieved
- documented actions and follow-up

This restores information symmetry between the three critical groups:

**management → board → shareholders.**

### *8.3.5 Principle 5: Incentives Must Support Purpose and MCOs*

Incentive design is a form of system programming.

If incentives conflict with purpose or MCOs, culture inevitably fails.

PDG requires that:

- Executive compensation aligns to MCO performance.
- Ethical and cultural indicators influence reward.
- Risk-adjusted performance metrics replace volume-only targets.

This prevents the Wells Fargo, Boeing, Wirecard, 2008 Global Financial Crisis failures, and tens of thousands like them from repeating.

### *8.3.6 Principle 6: Assurance Must Verify Truth, Not Controls*

Traditional internal audit provides assurance on some internal controls. Risk groups provide risk lists and risk heatmaps.

PDG requires assurance on **mission-critical truth**.

OCRUM gives internal audit and other assurance providers a new mandate:

- Verify the reliability of MCO reporting.
- Validate MCO uncertainty/risk assessments.
- Assess cultural risk indicators.
- Test the systems designed to ensure truthful escalation.

This redefines assurance as the evidence engine that supports fiduciary duty.

#### *8.3.7 Principle 7: Oversight Must Operate as a Closed Loop*

Engineering systems rely on closed loops: measure → compare → correct → verify.

PDG applies this logic directly:

1. **Define board purpose, including MCO oversight**
2. **Define entity purpose and MCOs**
3. **Assess uncertainty/risk**
4. **Report insights to the board**
5. **Board challenges, adjusts, and directs**
6. **Management responds and mitigates**
7. **Assurance verifies reliability**
8. **Board revisits and recalibrates**

This loop prevents drift, blind spots, and cultural silence.

### 8.4 How PDG and OCRUM Integrate into a Coherent System

PDG provides the **governance architecture**.

OCRUM provides the **operational engine**.

Together:

- PDG defines *what must be overseen.*
- OCRUM defines *how uncertainty/risk is continuously assessed.*
- Integrated reporting feeds *what the board sees.*
- Assurance verifies *what the board can trust.*
- Incentive alignment shapes *how people behave.*

The result is a governance system capable of early detection, informed decision-making, and resilience under uncertainty.

This is the scientific antidote to the Quadrillion-Dollar Problem.

### 8.5 The PDG Strategic Blueprint Illustrated

**Purpose → MCOs → Uncertainty → Reporting → Oversight → Action → Assurance → Learning → Adaptation**

This sequence forms a tight, evidence-based oversight cycle.

Unlike traditional governance, PDG:

- begins with purpose – entity and board;
- centres on MCOs;
- integrates risk into performance;
- escalates unfiltered truth on risk/uncertainty;
- assures information reliability;
- creates real accountability; and
- links reward to mission-critical outcomes.

It is the first governance model that functions like a modern control system.

## 8.6 Why This Blueprint Is the Only Scalable Answer to the Quadrillion-Dollar Problem

### *8.6.1 It Addresses the Root Causes, Not Symptoms*

PDG eliminates:

- the Purpose Void
- the Don't Tell/Don't Ask Syndrome
- Mission-Critical Blindness
- compliance-centric ERM
- ineffective, culturally harmful controls centric traditional internal audit
- politically filtered reporting
- cultural suppression
- oversight theatre

### *8.6.2 It Synthesizes Strategy, Governance, Risk, and Assurance*

PDG is the first model that makes these functions interdependent—not siloed.

### *8.6.3 It Works across All Sectors*

Whether in banking, healthcare, manufacturing, energy, tech, charities/NFP (Not-For-Profit), or government, the structural failures are identical.

PDG's architecture fits them all.

#### *8.6.4 It Scales from Startups to Large Multinationals*

The number of MCOs changes; level of risk assessment rigour varies; the architecture does not.

### 8.7 From Blueprint to Execution: What Comes Next

PDG and OCRUM give boards and executives the conceptual and operational architecture.

The next step is **implementation**, which requires:

- board adoption of board purpose
- identification and mapping of MCOs
- design of objective-centric reporting
- creation of an OCRUM engine
- redesign of assurance roles
- incentive alignment
- cultural rewiring
- technology and analytics support

Subsequent chapters will walk through the practical playbook for replacing legacy governance with PDG—turning a conceptual blueprint into a functioning, measurable oversight system.

### 8.8 Conclusion:– The Future of Governance Is Engineered

The Quadrillion-Dollar Problem is not caused by bad people.

It is caused by bad systems—legacy governance architectures and methods that make failure predictable.

PDG and OCRUM offer the first scientifically structured alternative:

a governance system built for uncertainty, aligned to purpose, centred on mission-critical outcomes, linked to performance, and powered by reliable information.

The blueprint is here.

The question is whether leaders will use it—or allow the failures of the past to define the future.

# PART IV

# The Implementation Blueprint

Purpose in Practice

# 9

# Defining Board Purpose

## The First Step towards Accountability

*A board without a stated purpose is a compass without a north.*

### 9.1 Introduction: Why Board Purpose Is the Missing Foundation

Across jurisdictions, frameworks, and governance codes, one striking omission persists:

**Boards are not required to define their purpose and few do.**[1]

Companies define mission and vision.

Management teams define strategy.

But most boards—the group legally responsible for governance, oversight, accountability, and trust—operate without a written statement of *why they exist* and *whom they serve.*

This absence is not benign.

It is the root of:

- inconsistent oversight;
- misaligned priorities;
- weak accountability;
- fragmented committee structures;
- performative governance;
- Mission-Critical Blindness; and
- the Don't Tell/Don't Ask Syndrome.

Purpose-Driven Governance (PDG) begins with a foundational act of clarity:

**Boards must explicitly define, approve, disclose, and operationalize their Purpose.**

This chapter provides the blueprint.

DOI: 10.1201/9781003685753-13

## 9.2 Why Defining Board Purpose Is Essential for Modern Governance

### *9.2.1 Purpose Anchors Oversight*

Without a declared purpose, board decision-making becomes reactive and inconsistent.

Purpose creates a unifying oversight agenda.

### *9.2.2 Purpose Aligns Directors to a Common Duty*

Directors bring different backgrounds, assumptions, and biases.

Explicit purpose creates a shared north star, reducing misinterpretation and cognitive drift.

### *9.2.3 Purpose Protects the Board under Modern Legal Expectations*

Delaware's Caremark jurisprudence direction is clear:

Boards must oversee the systems that ensure mission-critical performance, safety, compliance, and reporting integrity.

A defined board purpose clarifies **what** the board is responsible for ensuring—and **what evidence** they require.

### *9.2.4 Purpose Improves Stakeholder Trust*

Investors and regulators now expect boards to explain:

- what is it they safeguard;
- how they create value through oversight; and
- how they prevent catastrophic blind spots.

Board purpose becomes the foundation of trustworthiness.

## 9.3 What a Board Purpose Statement Must Contain

A Board Purpose Statement is not marketing language.

It is a governance instrument with five required elements:

1. **Why the board exists** (its core oversight mandate)
2. **Whom the board serves** (shareholders, entity, stakeholders, or a defined combination)

3. **What the board must ensure** (Mission-Critical Objectives (MCOs) linked to purpose)
4. **How the board exercises oversight** (information, challenge, assurance, culture)
5. **How the board holds itself accountable** (evaluation and improvement)

A strong Board Purpose Statement eliminates ambiguity and provides a structural basis for PDG.

### 9.4 The Step-by-Step Method for Drafting a Board Purpose Statement

The process has six steps. Each step builds alignment, clarity, and credibility.

#### *9.4.1 Step 1: Identify the Enterprise's Purpose and MCOs*

A board cannot define its purpose until it understands:

- the organization's fundamental purpose;
- the MCOs required to fulfil that purpose; and
- boards are now expected to oversee risk/uncertainty linked to MCOs.

This provides the raw material for the board's governance mandate.

#### *9.4.2 Step 2: Facilitate a Director Workshop on Board Purpose*

This workshop should explore four questions:

1. **Why does our board exist?**
2. **What outcomes must we ensure?**
3. **Who do we serve, and in what order of priority?**
4. **What systems do we need to obtain reliable information on MCO risk?**

The workshop reveals differences in assumptions, expectations, and mental models.

#### *9.4.3 Step 3: Draft the Board Purpose Statement*

A first draft should follow a simple structure. For example:

> *The purpose of the Board of Directors is to ensure that the organization fulfills its defined purpose by overseeing the setting and achievement of its Mission-Critical Objectives, monitoring uncertainty and risk that threaten those objectives, ensuring the reliability of information provided to the Board, and holding management accountable for ethical, lawful, and performance-driven execution.*

This is not final; it is the starting point for refinement.

#### *9.4.4 Step 4: Refine through Governance Committee Review*

The Governance Committee ensures that the statement:

- is consistent with law and fiduciary requirements;
- aligns with enterprise purpose;
- connects directly to oversight duties;
- is specific, not aspirational; and
- embeds PDG principles.

This step transforms the draft into an actionable governance artefact.

#### *9.4.5 Step 5: Approve through Full Board Resolution*

Approval should be formal and minuted.

Directors should affirm that the Purpose Statement defines:

- the board's reason for being—its purpose;
- the purpose of their core duties;
- the oversight scope;
- the information they require; and
- the evidence necessary to demonstrate good-faith oversight.

This moment marks the board's explicit commitment to oversight integrity.

#### 9.4.6 *Step 6: Disclose the Purpose Statement Externally*

Public disclosure increases:

- transparency
- trust
- accountability

It signals to investors, regulators, employees, and society what the board stands for—and how it will measure its performance.

### 9.5 Embedding Board Purpose into Governance Infrastructure

Defining purpose is the beginning.

Embedding purpose makes it real.

#### 9.5.1 *Integration into Board and Committee Charters*

Every charter should be rewritten to align with board purpose and MCOs.

For example:

- Audit Committee → Oversight of uncertainty/risk linked to reliable/GAAP compliant financial disclosures
- Strategy and Value Oversight Committee → Oversight of uncertainty/risk linked to all other MCOs
- Human Resources/Compensation → Incentives aligned to purpose and MCOs and MCO risk/status reporting
- Governance Committee → Culture, director capability, purpose evaluation

Charters become operational documents—not ceremonial ones.

#### 9.5.2 *Embedding Purpose into Board Agendas*

Agendas should anchor every meeting around:

- MCO status including current/past performance
- uncertainty and emerging risks and opportunities
- culture indicators

- assurance findings
- strategic decisions linked to purpose

PDG agendas eliminate random walk governance—the common practice of drifting from topic to topic without strategic coherence.

#### *9.5.3 Embedding Purpose into Decision Protocols*

Boards should require every proposal to include:

- purpose alignment
- impact on MCOs
- uncertainty/risk analysis
- assurance implications
- cultural considerations
- long-term value impact

Decisions become consistent and evidence-based.

#### *9.5.4 Embedding Purpose into Board Evaluations*

Board effectiveness reviews must assess:

- how well the board fulfilled its purpose
- quality of MCO risk oversight
- rigour of information challenge
- independence of thought
- cultural impact
- responsiveness to early warning signals

Purpose becomes the metric—not meeting attendance.

### 9.6 How Board Purpose Reduces Legal and Fiduciary Exposure

#### *9.6.1 It Clarifies the Board's Oversight Duty under Caremark*

Clear purpose + structured oversight of MCOs = demonstrable good faith/duty of care.

*9.6.2 It Creates Evidence of Intentional Oversight*

Minutes, charters, and reporting systems aligned to purpose create a legally defensible oversight trail.

*9.6.3 It Improves D&O Insurability*

Insurers, going forward as board director fiduciary duty of care is codified, may require evidence of:

- strategic oversight
- objective-centric reporting
- culture health
- MCO risk management

A Board Purpose Statement becomes a key underwriting artefact.

### 9.7 A Model Board Purpose Statement (PDG-Compliant)

Boards may adapt this template to their context:

> *The purpose of the Board of Directors is to ensure the organization fulfills its stated purpose by overseeing the achievement of its Mission-Critical Objectives; ensuring the reliability of performance, risk, and cultural information presented to the Board; monitoring Mission Critical uncertainty and emerging threats; ensuring management's actions align with purpose and values; and securing long-term enterprise resilience, trust, and value for those we serve.*

This is the core of PDG made explicit.

### 9.8 Conclusion: Accountability Begins with Purpose

A board cannot be accountable for what it has not defined.

A board cannot govern what it cannot describe.

And a board cannot protect what it cannot see.

Purpose is not a slogan.

It is the foundation of legitimacy, authority, and fiduciary accountability.

Defining board purpose is the **first practical step** towards solving the Quadrillion-Dollar Problem—and the gateway to the integrated PDG–OCRUM model introduced in earlier chapters.

In the chapters ahead, the book moves from purpose definition to **full implementation**:

designing MCO registers, establishing OCRUM reporting systems, integrating assurance streams, and building technology-enabled governance platforms that make PDG real, repeatable, and measurable.

## Notes

1 For more details on importance of clear board purpose see author's LinkedIn post "Is real root cause of governance failures in quadrillions of dollars a lack of agreement on PURPOSE of governance? ChatGPT and I say YES": www.linkedin.com/posts/tim-leech-01950013_is-real-root-cause-of-governance-failures-activity-7343608446866407425-UTjf/

Re how many boards disclose board purpose see my LinkedIn post "Most agree – effective boards are key to good governance. Yet <1% companies agree/disclose BOARD PURPOSE. Risk/IA have to guess their PURPOSE": www.linkedin.com/posts/tim-leech-01950013_most-agree-effective-boards-are-key-to-activity-7325127156781518849-tNoB/

# 10

# Identifying and Monitoring Mission-Critical Objectives (MCOs)

*Entity purpose becomes real only when linked to the mission critical objectives that determine survival and success.*

## 10.1 Introduction: Why Mission-Critical Objectives (MCOs) Are the Heart of Modern Governance

No idea is more foundational to Purpose-Driven Governance (PDG) and OCRUM than this:

**Boards cannot oversee purpose—nor protect the enterprise—unless they know which objectives matter most.**

MCOs are not ordinary goals.

They are the **small set of outcomes whose failure could threaten the organization's viability, integrity, or strategic future and success.**

They are the enterprise's:

- **value-preservation foundations** (e.g. safety, liquidity, reporting integrity, compliance)
- **value-creation engines** (e.g. strategic transformations, critical product launches, high-stakes investments)

Every corporate crisis examined in Chapters 4–6 began with one truth:

**The board did not know which objectives were mission-critical—or lacked reliable information on their risk/uncertainty status.**

This chapter provides the technical blueprint for fixing that permanently.

DOI: 10.1201/9781003685753-14

## 10.2 What Makes an Objective "Mission-Critical"?

Not all objectives carry equal weight.

MCOs are those whose failure results in:

### *10.2.1 Existential Threats*

- loss of life or safety failure
- loss of regulatory license
- catastrophic legal exposure
- insolvency or liquidity collapse

### *10.2.2 Strategic Failure*

- collapse of a major transformation
- breakdown of core product/service integrity
- inability to spot and respond to major business model change
- inability to achieve a value-defining milestone

### *10.2.3 Integrity Failure*

- unreliable financial reporting
- severe cultural or ethical breakdown
- serious illegality
- deliberate concealment or information distortion

### *10.2.4 Trust Failure*

- reputational damage
- customer abandonment
- investor or regulator intervention

If an objective's failure could appear on the front page of a newspaper—or in a future Caremark or country equivalent investor/stakeholder lawsuit—it is almost certainly mission-critical.

## 10.3 The MCO Identification Process: A Practical Blueprint

The MCO Identification Process uses seven structured steps aligned to PDG and OCRUM.

#### *10.3.1 Step 1: Clarify Organizational Purpose*

Entity purpose, defined in Section 9.4.1 as part of defining board purpose, sets the foundation.

MCOs are the **objectives most essential to delivering entity purpose.**

#### *10.3.2 Step 2: Inventory All Strategic and Operational Objectives*

Most organizations have dozens—even hundreds—of objectives embedded in:

- strategic plans
- annual budgets
- business unit scorecards
- regulatory obligations
- operational KPIs
- job descriptions
- executive compensation plans

The goal is **not** to manage all of them at the board level.

The goal is to **sort the many into the few** that are mission-critical.

#### *10.3.3 Step 3: Classify Objectives into Categories*

PDG and OCRUM classify objectives using a simple taxonomy:

1. **MCOs/Board-Critical Objectives**
2. **Important but Not Mission-Critical**
3. **Operational/Management-Level Objectives**

This classification reduces noise and focuses oversight.

#### *10.3.4 Step 4: Apply the Mission-Critical Test*

Each potential MCO is evaluated using four screening questions:

1. **Would failure of this objective materially threaten the purpose of the enterprise?**
2. **Would failure cause severe harm to customers, employees, regulators, society, or investors?**

3. **Would failure significantly impair strategy, financial integrity, or license to operate?**
4. **Would/could the board be held accountable—legally or reputationally—if this objective failed and board couldn't demonstrate oversight?**

Objectives scoring "yes" on multiple questions become MCO candidates.

#### *10.3.5 Step 5: Validate MCOs with Cross-Functional Leadership*

Validation includes executives from:

- operations
- finance
- risk
- safety
- legal
- compliance
- internal audit
- HR/culture
- strategy

This ensures the board sees the full landscape of mission-critical risk and opportunity.

#### *10.3.6 Step 6: Board Review and Approval of Final CEO Proposed MCO Set*

A board typically ends with 10–15 **MCOs**, depending on size and complexity.

Examples:

- **Safety and quality integrity**
- **Reliable financial reporting**
- **Liquidity and capital resilience**
- **Cybersecurity and data integrity**
- **Regulatory compliance and legal obligations**
- **Culture, ethics, and trust**
- **Major strategic value creation objectives**

The board resolution should explicitly state:

**These are the objectives we will monitor with enhanced rigor.**

### *10.3.7 Step 7: Create the MCO Register*

The MCO Register is the central governance document and information repository linking:

- entity purpose
- MCO definition/oversight
- decisions on target risk/uncertainty assessment rigour
- key performance indicators
- uncertainty and risk factors
- early warning indicators
- risk velocity and exposure
- management accountability for risk status reporting
- assurance requirements
- reporting frequency to the board

It is the engine of PDG and OCRUM.

## 10.4 Building the MCO Register: The Technical Blueprint

Getting started is simple. A five-step overview with core decision required on each MCO is shown in Figure 10.1[1]:

Step 2 includes a very important decision few companies or boards make today – the target level of risk/uncertainty assessment rigour. Target risk assessment rigour levels selected directly impacts reliability of risk/uncertainty status reports that go to the board. A simplified guide to risk assessment rigour is shown in Figure 10.2. In most companies today, the most common choice for mission critical risk assessment rigour already made is "Not Assigned." Not defining the level of risk assessment rigour is one of the least discussed understood risks to better governance.

The core building block of OCRUM, UncertaintyStatusline© assessment method is shown in Figure 10.3. Every assessment integrates objective/threats to achievement/opportunities/risk treatments/

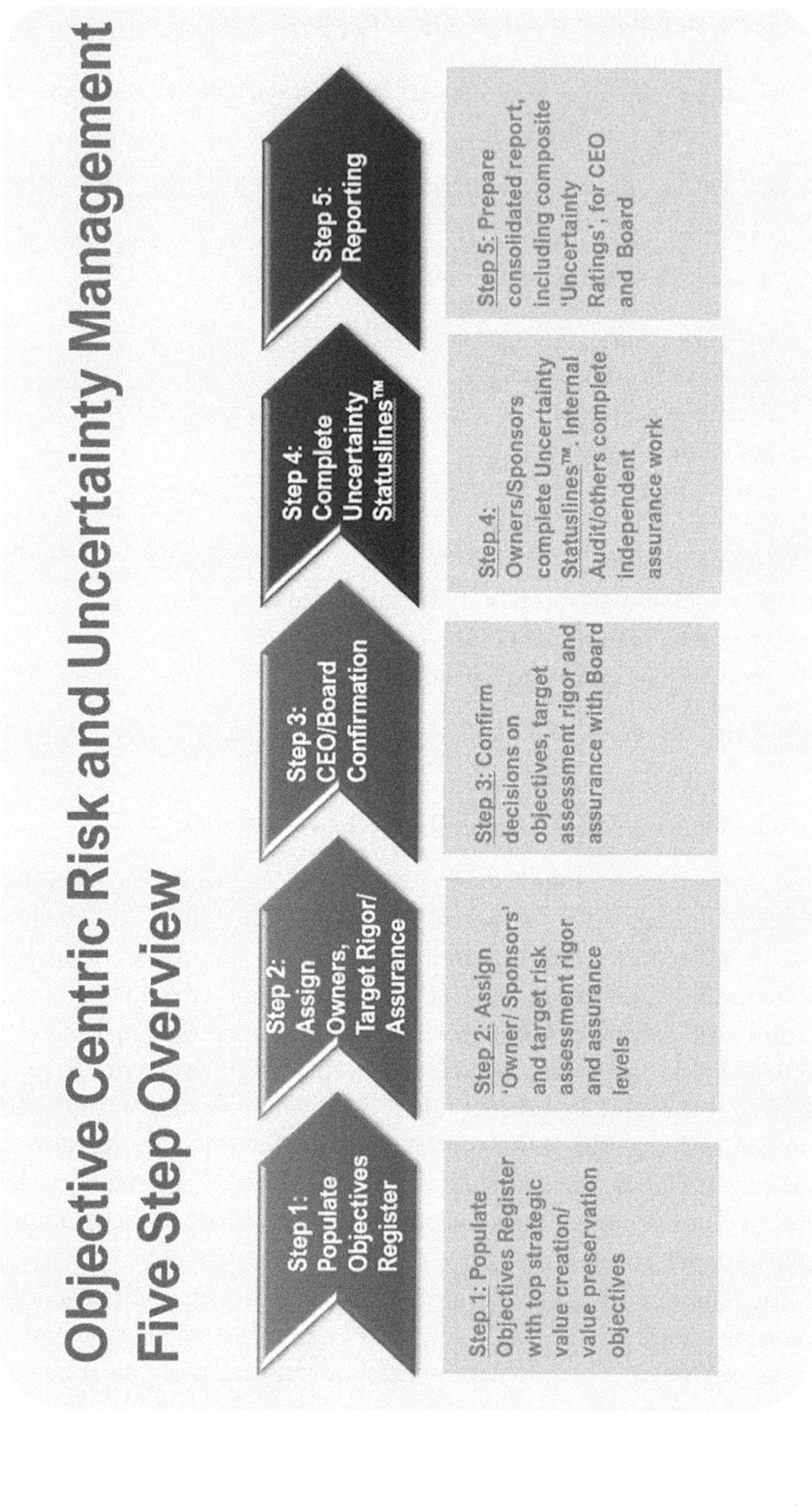


**Figure 10.1** OCRUM Five-Step Overview.

## Risk Assessment Rigour ("RAR") User Guide

| RAR LEVEL | DESCRIPTION |
|---|---|
| Not Assigned (NA) |   |
| Not Rated (NR) |  |
| Intuitive/Experiential | 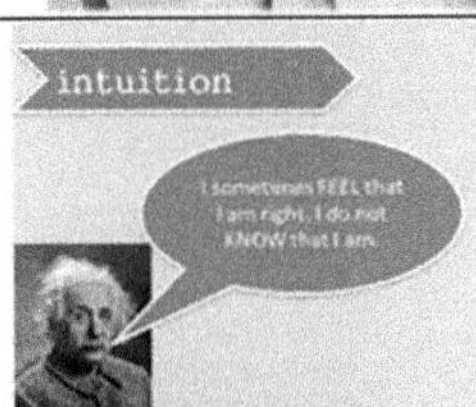  |
| Traffic Light/Time Limited |  |
| Full Risk/Risk Treatment Assessment | More work and time required to identify risks, risk treatments, RESIDUAL RISK STATUS information, and COMPOSITE RESIDUAL RISK RATING. |
| High (H) | Quite a bit more work and time reserved for very important objectives |
| Very High (VH) | A lot of work and time required reserved for absolutely the most important objectives. |
| Very High + (VH+) | This amount of effort and time is reserved for situation where there is a desire to be as certain as humanly possible. |

**Figure 10.2** Risk Assessment Rigour (RAR) User Guide.

residual risk status data including performance, impact of not achieving the objective, concerns, impediments, and management's uncertainty/risk acceptance decision. Once initial risk/uncertainty acceptability decision has been made, analysis can be extended to include assessing whether current Risk Treatment Strategy is "OPTIMIZED"—lowest cost possible combination of risk treatments that produces

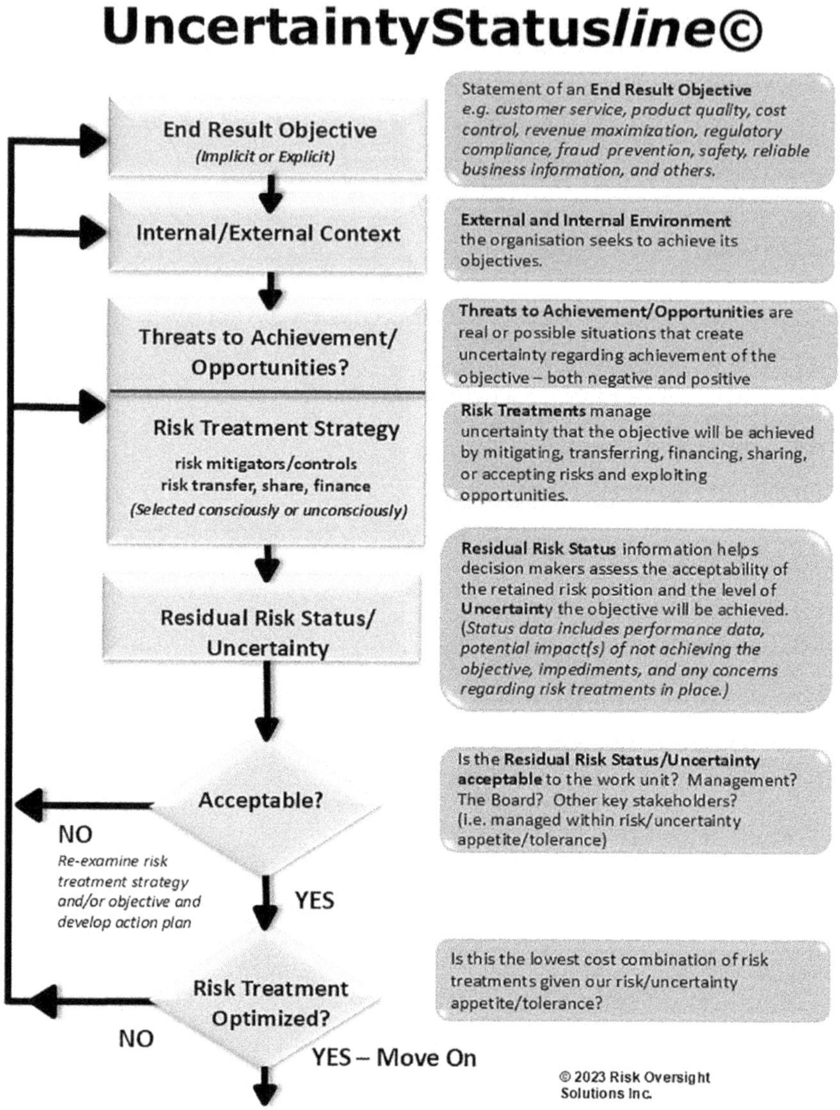


**Figure 10.3** UncertaintyStatusline©.

an acceptable residual risk/uncertainty status. Core taxonomy used in UncertaintyStatusline© aligns with ISO 31000 and COSO ERM, with the exception of RESIDUAL RISK/UNCERTAINTY STATUS. It is unique to UncertaintyStatusline©. The data sets in this step have been selected to help OWNER/SPONSORS, and those

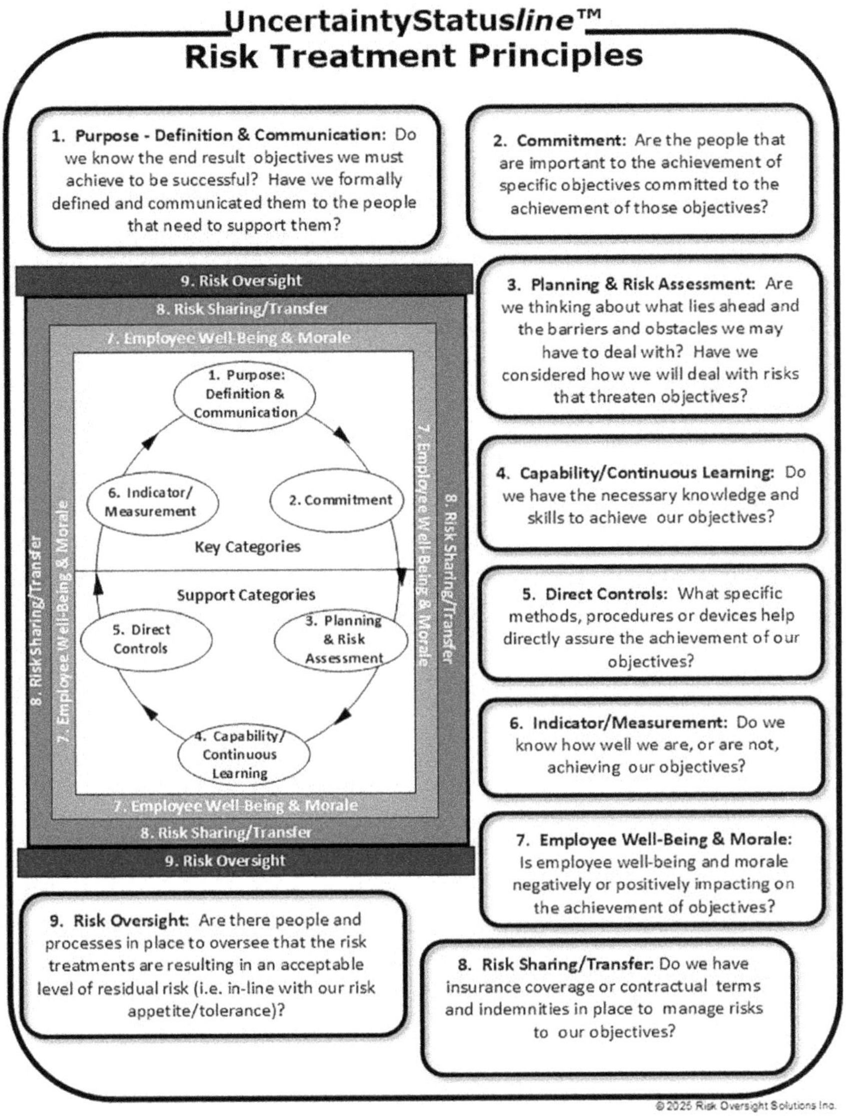


**Figure 10.4** UncertaintyStatusline© Risk Treatment Principles.

that oversee them, with most relevant information needed to make a decision on risk/uncertainty acceptability.

Risk assessments can be guided by nine-category RISK TREATMENT PRINCIPLES framework shown in Figure 10.4. It is supported by over 100 specific risk treatment elements that can be used to build risk treatment portfolios.[2]

## 10.5 The MCO Dashboard: Turning Information into Actionable Insight

The MCO Dashboard that flows from the MCO process described in Section 10.4 provides the board with a **visual, real-time summary** of:

- MCOs
- MCO target and actual risk assessment rigour
- MCO Uncertainty/risk acceptability rating (NOTE: a full assessment should also be available as an optional supplement)
- Current/past MCO performance
- uncertainty exposure/impact of not achieving MCO
- assurance ratings, if any, on the MCO risk/uncertainty status being reported.

Unlike dashboards overloaded with KPIs, the MCO Dashboard includes only-MCOs (Figure 10.5). It can be customized to each company. Senior management and board can elect to see the full analysis that supports the UncertaintyStatus Ratings assigned, and can require CROs and CAEs to provide commentary. Summary performance data for each MCO should be included.

**Core Objectives**

| Mission Critical Objectives | Owner/Sponsor | Uncertainty |
|---|---|---|
| *Achieve 8% return on private equite investments in excess of sector benchmarks* | Mary Brown | |
| Increase customer retention by 15% year over year. | Chuck Smith | |
| Increase customer satisfaction from 3.2/5 to 4.0/5 by year end | Elaine Ford | |
| Reduce lost time due to accidents by 30% year over year. | Glenn Goucher | |

**Uncertainty Ratings (URs)**

| | |
|---|---|
| | Fully acceptable level of uncertainty of achievement. Any significant concerns have been identified and shared upwards |
| | Some management effort is required to reduce uncertainty of achievement to an acceptable level. |
| | Considerable management action is required to reduce uncertainty of achievement to an acceptable level. |
| | Significant analysis and corrective action by Senior Management and the Board is urgently required to reduce uncertainty of achievement to an acceptable level. |
| | Massive corrective action by Senior Management and the Board is required now to reduce uncertainty of achievement to an acceptable level. |

**Figure 10.5** Mission Critical Objectives Overview and Uncertainty Rating Definitions.

## 10.6 How Boards Should Monitor MCOs

PDG requires a structured oversight rhythm.

### *10.6.1 Quarterly MCO Deep Dives*

Each quarter, the board should deep-dive:

- one to three MCOs
- uncertainty profile
- assurance results
- major shifts
- management plans
- resource needs

This replaces scattershot reporting with structured oversight.

### *10.6.2 Real-Time Escalation of Red Flags*

Boards must call for and receive immediate alerts if:

- an MCO moves to a high/red unacceptable uncertainty rating;
- emerging risks linked to MCOs with potential to materially affect achievement accelerate;
- cultural indicators linked to data reliability decline; and
- risk/uncertainty status data reliability becomes uncertain.

This eliminates the "surprise factor" at the next board meeting.

### *10.6.3 Annual Re-Validation of the MCO Set*

Periodically, management and the board reassesses decisions on MCOs:

- strategic changes
- new regulatory focus/risks
- changing market realities
- lessons from assurance
- new uncertainties
- performance changes

This ensures the MCOs set evolves with the enterprise.

### 10.7 How OCRUM Complements and Powers MCO Oversight

OCRUM provides the analytical engine for MCO monitoring:

- structured uncertainty assessments
- integrated MCO risk views
- scenario analysis
- stress testing
- risk velocity and exposure quantification
- assurance on information reliability

OCRUM transforms the MCOs Register from a list into a dynamic risk and assurance system.

### 10.8 MCOs and Legal Accountability: The Caremark Connection

Delaware courts have signalled it expect boards to oversee:

- mission-critical safety
- reliable disclosures
- culture and ethics
- compliance integrity
- strategic objectives that could drive illegality/unethical conduct (e.g. Wells Fargo)

Formal MCO oversight:

- creates documented evidence of good-faith governance
- reduces exposure in shareholder derivative actions
- improves D&O insurability
- satisfies investor expectations for structured oversight

Boards that don't oversee MCOs/risk are legally vulnerable, at least in the United States. Boards with MCOs/risk process—and documented oversight—have structural protection.

### 10.9 Practical Examples: How MCOs Differ by Industry

**Financial Institutions**

- Liquidity
- Credit integrity

- AML/financial crime compliance
- Model risk
- Reliable financial disclosure

**Healthcare**

- Patient safety
- Clinical quality
- Regulatory compliance
- Data integrity

**Aviation and Transportation**

- Safety systems
- Engineering integrity
- Crew training and culture

**Technology**

- Cybersecurity
- Data privacy
- AI safety
- Platform trust

**Manufacturing**

- Product quality
- Worker safety
- Supply chain integrity

Each MCO flows from purpose.
Every MCO is existential.

### 10.10 Conclusion: MCOs Turn Purpose into Measurable Oversight

Purpose without MCOs is philosophy.

MCOs without structured risk/uncertainty oversight are blind spots.

MCOs without OCRUM are guesswork.

Together, PDG + OCRUM + MCOs create the **core** of 21st-century governance:

- clear oversight focus
- real-time insight

- performance focus
- early detection
- transparency
- assurance
- accountability

In the chapters ahead, this book will show how to implement integrated reporting, assurance mapping, cultural monitoring, and technology-enabled governance platforms that bring MCO oversight to life—replacing oversight theatre with oversight reality.

## Notes

1 This visual and many others in this section are available free at: https://riskoversightsolutions.com/resources/ They are the product of 40 years of evolution and global testing across all business sectors, public sector and not-for-profits.

2 Full details on risk treatment principles, elements and trigger questions designed to help management, risk and internal audit complete effective assessments are available free at: https://riskoversightsolutions.com/wp-content/uploads/2023/09/UncertaintyStatusline-Risk-Treatment-Principles-and-Trigger-Questions.pdf_1695402956.pdf

# 11

# Quantifying and Reporting Uncertainty/Risk

*Boards need reports on uncertainty/risk linked to MCOs – and reports on reliability of what's in those reports.*

## 11.1 Introduction: Why Uncertainty Must Become Measurable

For most of corporate history, boards have treated uncertainty as a qualitative concept—described with words like *high, low, moderate, emerging, trending,* or *under control.* These descriptors are subjective, unstructured, and heavily filtered by cognitive biases and internal politics.

This approach collapses under modern complexity.

The core argument of PDG and OCRUM is simple:

**If a board doesn't receive reliable reports on uncertainty/risk linked to Mission-Critical Objectives (MCOs), it cannot govern the organization responsibly.**

This chapter introduces two essential tools:

1. **The Acceptable/Unacceptable Uncertainty Model (AU/UU)**
   - a structured way to measure and communicate uncertainty linked directly to each MCO and make decisions needed.
2. **The Board Assurance Index (BAI)**
   - a single, evidence-based measure on level of assurance on risk/uncertainty information linked to MCOs the board receives.

Together, AU/UU and BAI replace vague risk language with quantified risk oversight clarity.

DOI: 10.1201/9781003685753-15

## 11.2 The Problem: Boards Receive Heat Maps and Reports on Internal Control Deficiencies, Not MCO Uncertainty Status

Traditional reporting tools fail for three reasons:

### *11.2.1 They Categorize Risks, Not Uncertainties*

Most systems describe risks as discrete threats ("cyber attack," "talent shortage," "market decline") rather than assessing **how uncertainty of multiple threats/opportunities could affect achievement of each MCO.**

### *11.2.2 They Treat Consequences and Likelihood as Fixed*

Reality is dynamic, but heat maps are static snapshots.

### *11.2.3 They Ignore Data Reliability*

Boards see risk scores—but not how confident management is in underlying assessments, assumptions, and data being presented. Dedicated risk functions and internal audit rarely assess/report on risk/uncertainty linked to MCOs. Most aren't allowed to.

AU/UU and BAI solve these flaws.

## Part I: The AU/UU Model

## 11.3 The AU/UU Model: A Simple, Scientific Way to Report Uncertainty

The AU/UU model makes uncertainty actionable by placing uncertainty affecting an MCO into one of two categories:

- **AU:**
  Uncertainty levels deemed acceptable. All significant concerns/risks being accepted have been shared upward.
- **UU —four levels:**
  Four levels of UU seen as outside entity/CEO risk appetite.

The primary classification is binary on purpose—boards need clarity on management's risk acceptance decisions, not ambiguity. AU means management has no plans to make any changes to risk treatments or the objective. It does not mean there are no big risks being accepted. It does mean all risk acceptance decisions, if significant, have been shared with CEO and board.

### 11.4 How the AU/UU Model Works

The model uses four steps:

**Step 1—Define the Objective**
Every AU/UU assessment begins with a clearly defined MCO.

**Step 2—Establish Objective Tolerances**
For each MCO, management, ideally with board input, should define, or at least consider:

- **Performance tolerance** (how far off-target is acceptable)
- **Time tolerance** (how long the deviation can persist)
- **Risk/uncertainty tolerance** (how much uncertainty and performance variability can be absorbed before success and entity purpose is threatened)

**Step 3—Identify Significant Threats to Achievement/ Opportunities and Risk Treatments**
Both upside and downside uncertainties are considered, including risks/opportunities linked to:

- operational variability
- market forces
- geopolitical developments
- system integrity
- reliance on/use of AI
- cultural dynamics
- compliance pressure
- technological disruption

**Step 4—Paint a Picture of Current Residual Risk Status/ Uncertainty**
This needs to include:

- information on risks being accepted, in whole or part (Concerns—Acceptable and Concerns Unacceptable)
- opportunities available and their status
- impact of not achieving MCO
- best available performance information
- any impediments that block management from modifying current risk treatments

**Step 5—Owner/Sponsor decision—Classify Uncertainty as AU or one of four levels of UU**

Using:

- magnitude
- likelihood
- velocity
- interdependence
- early warning indicators
- potential impact on MCO
- potential impact on entity and share price
- potential impact on management compensation

Uncertainty is then placed in one of two primary categories—AU or UU, if it is UN then a decision on how unacceptable current uncertainty/risk is required to communicate urgency and escalation requirements:

**AU = Uncertainty we are willing to accept/tolerate. No additional risk treatments needed right now.**

**UU = Uncertainty that requires action, escalation or, at the highest level, possible board intervention. There are four levels of UU. See Figure 11.1.**

**Uncertainty Ratings (URs)**

| |
|---|
| Fully acceptable level of uncertainty of achievement. Any significant concerns have been identified and shared upwards |
| Some management effort is required to reduce uncertainty of achievement to an acceptable level. |
| Considerable management action is required to reduce uncertainty of achievement to an acceptable level. |
| Significant analysis and corrective action by Senior Management and the Board is urgently required to reduce uncertainty of achievement to an acceptable level. |
| Massive corrective action by Senior Management and the Board is required now to reduce uncertainty of achievement to an acceptable level. |

**Figure 11.1** Acceptable and Unacceptable Uncertainty Rating Definition.

This classification becomes the centrepiece of MCO reporting.

## 11.5 Why AU/UU Is Superior to Traditional Risk Scoring

### *11.5.1 It Is Decision-Oriented*

Instead of debating numbers, the board discusses management's decisions on whether uncertainty status is **acceptable** or **unacceptable**. If it is unacceptable, how far outside of acceptable risk tolerance is it, how urgent is it that it be addressed, and how high up should the status be escalated for decisions/actions.

### *11.5.2 It Integrates Performance and Risk*

AU/UU ties uncertainty directly to actual and expected results—not theoretical hazards.

### *11.5.3 It Eliminates the Illusion of Precision*

Boards no longer mistake colour-coded risk maps for truth.

### *11.5.4 It Is Legally Defensible*

AU/UU aligns with Caremark expectations because it explicitly documents active management and board oversight of risk linked to MCOs. It is supported by the BUSINESS JUDGMENT RULE when done in good faith. Business judgment rule specifics are being improved in some jurisdictions to support board engagement in decisions linked to acceptable risk/uncertainty linked to MCOs.

## Part II: The BAI

## 11.6 The Missing Dimension: Confidence in the Information Itself

One of the most dangerous blind spots in governance is the assumption that information on risk/uncertainty provided to the board is relevant, accurate, reliable, and unbiased.

Experience—and the case studies in Chapters 4–6—prove otherwise.

Boards often receive information that is:

- incomplete
- not linked to MCOs
- filtered
- sanitized
- politically shaped
- based on weak data
- lacking independent assurance

Without a measure of confidence, any assessment of uncertainty is incomplete.

### 11.7 Introducing the BAI

The BAI quantifies how much confidence the board should place in the risk/uncertainty status information supporting management's AU/UU decision/classification for each MCO.

It is simple, intuitive, and evidence-based. It is derived from decisions on Target Risk Assessment Rigour and Target Assurance Levels outlined in Chapter 10 in step 2 of OCRUM implementation steps.

Each MCO receives a BAI score from 1 to 5, based on four dimensions:

**Dimension 1: Data Quality and Reliability**

- Is the risk and performance data complete, timely, accurate, and independently verified?
- Is the assessment/reporting system structured or ad hoc/intuitive and experiential?

**Dimension 2: Management's Expertise and Judgment**

- Are the assessments prepared by subject-matter experts with/without expert assistance?
- Are they free from optimism bias and political pressure?

**Dimension 3: Assurance Coverage**

- Has internal audit, risk, compliance, safety, or external auditors provided assurance on this MCO risk/uncertainty status report?
- Is assurance recent and objective?
- How rigorous was the quality assurance audit/review?

**Dimension 4: Escalation Integrity and Culture**

- Do people feel safe reporting bad news?
- Does evidence support the claim?

Each dimension is scored from 1 to 5. The composite score becomes the summarized five-level BAI.

### 11.8 Interpreting BAI Scores

BAI 5: High Assurance on uncertainty status (NOTE: that status may indicate very high residual risk/uncertainty is being accepted)

- Data reliable, verified, timely
- Strong assurance coverage
- Healthy speak-up culture
- Management provides unfiltered truth re uncertainty status

BAI 3–4: Moderate Assurance on uncertainty status

- Data generally reliable but with some gaps
- Assurance incomplete
- Cultural signals mixed
- Requires regular monitoring

BAI 1–2: Lower Confidence (Alert) on uncertainty status

- May be significant data reliability issues
- Weak or no assurance on reliability of risk status report
- Speak-up culture weak
- Higher filtering risk

AU with low BAI should be considered higher risk for decision making.

## Part III: Integrating AU/UU and BAI Into Board Reporting

### 11.9 The AU/UU + BAI Reporting Format

For each MCO, management reports:

1. **MCO performance update**
2. **Uncertainty status assessment**

3. **AU or one of four-level UU classifications**
4. **BAI score (1–5)**
5. **Assurance updates**
6. **Required board or committee action**

This entire MCO summary should fit on **one page per MCO**.

## 11.10 How Boards Can Use AU/UU and BAI in Practice

### *11.10.1 Prioritization*

- MCOs in high/red UU state are prioritized for deep dive.
- Low BAI scores signal MCOs where there is less assurance on uncertainty/risk status report.

### *11.10.2 Escalation*

- High/red UU conditions trigger rapid response.
- Low BAI alerts board to lower confidence the risk/uncertainty assessment and status report is reliable.

### *11.10.3 Accountability*

- When UU is rated high/red management must explain why and what they are doing about it, particularly when MCO performance is negative/below target.
- Low BAI scores indicate generally more CEO/board tolerance for unreliable risk/uncertainty status reports. There is a time/money cost associated with higher BAI ratings. Majority of boards today receive very little on risk/uncertainty status linked to MCOs—at any level of reliability. Most risk and internal audit groups are not equipped or allowed at most companies to assess/report on risk/uncertainty linked to MCOs
- Compensation committees can integrate BAI into incentive design.

### *11.10.4 Transparency*

Boards now have a clear, documented record of how they supervised uncertainty—an invaluable defence under legal scrutiny.

## Part IV: Why AU/UU + BAI Close the Failure Information Loop

### 11.11 They Break the Don't Tell/Don't Ask Syndrome

Low BAI scores alert boards' status report they are reviewing may not be reliable. It's a transparent management/board endorsed risk acceptance decision. UU classifications expose hidden risks where decisions on acceptability and risk treatments or adjustment to the objective wording are needed. Most boards are told little about the risk/uncertainty status linked to MCOs, and little about reliability of information they receive on MCO risk status from management, risk functions, and internal audit.

Uncertainty can no longer be disguised behind dashboards or narratives.

### 11.12 They Replace Subjectivity with Knowledge

Boards no longer rely on tone, confidence, or optimistic storylines.

They rely on structured, quantified and quality assured analysis.

### 11.13 They Support Purpose-Driven Governance

- Purpose → MCOs
- MCOs → Uncertainty
- Uncertainty → AU/four level UU
- Information Reliability → BAI
- Oversight → Assurance
- Action → Accountability

This is PDG in its purest form.

### 11.14 They Provide a Legally Defensible Oversight Trail

Courts, at least in the United States, now expect documented evidence of:

- structured information systems
- meaningful CEO and board oversight of MCOs/areas
- good-faith engagement with red flags

AU/four level UU + BAI provide that trail. It is important to note that the "BUSINESS JUDGEMENT RULE" protects management and boards when risk acceptance decisions, including risk acceptance decisions on target BAI, are made in good faith. A number of jurisdictions, including Texas and Arizona, have taken/are taking steps to clarify and strengthen business judgment rule to protect boards that receive risk reports on MCOs and act on that information in good faith.

### 11.15 Conclusion: The Future of Governance Is Quantified Uncertainty

Boards cannot govern using narrative alone.

They need:

- reliable MCO uncertainty/risk status information;
- classification of acceptability of risk/uncertainty;
- evidence;
- assurance; and
- assurance measurement.

The AU/four-level UU model and the BAI give boards the tools to govern uncertainty with engineering precision.

They close the Failure Information Loop.

They expose the Don't Tell/Don't Ask culture.

They prevent Mission-Critical Blindness.

And they transform PDG from theory into actionable oversight.

The next chapter will explain **how to build integrated reporting and assurance systems** that support AU/UU, BAI, and MCO oversight—turning quantified uncertainty into better decisions, better performance, and better governance. It doesn't need to be expensive. A working MCOs framework can be launched in under a month.

# 12

# Integrating Assurance

## From Siloed Comfort to Objective-Centric Confidence

*Assurance, when fragmented, produces comfort—not confidence.*

### 12.1 Introduction: The Assurance Paradox

In most organizations, assurance is abundant—but often meaningless.

Boards receive:

- internal audit reports;
- risk committee updates;
- compliance attestations;
- safety audits;
- cyber certifications; and
- external audit conclusions on internal control "effectiveness" and the financial statements.

Yet despite this flood of "assurance," boards often remain **blind to the reliability of the information they receive on Mission-Critical Objectives (MCOs).**

This is the **Assurance Paradox**:

**The more assurance functions an organization has, the less clarity the board often gains.**

Why?

Because assurance is siloed, compliance-centric, risk-centric, controls-focused, and disconnected from the organization's purpose and MCOs.

PDG and OCRUM solve this paradox through a new model as follows.

DOI: 10.1201/9781003685753-16

#### *12.1.1 Integrated Objective-Centric Assurance (IOCA)*

A unified assurance architecture that:

- eliminates duplication;
- closes blind spots;
- provides independent verification of MCO reporting;
- supports AU/four-level UU classification and decision making;
- strengthens BAI scores; and
- enables demonstrable fiduciary duty of care oversight.

### 12.2 Why Traditional Assurance Fails Boards

#### *12.2.1 Siloed Mandates Create Fragmented Insight*

Internal audit focuses on internal controls.

Compliance focuses on rules.

Risk focuses on creating/reporting risk lists.

Safety focuses on incidents.

External audit focuses on binary opinions on financial reporting and controls.

No one owns **mission-critical truth**.

#### *12.2.2 Assurance Rarely Links to MCOs*

Assurance providers do not report:

- "Is the MCO at risk?"
- "Is the information on MCO risk/uncertainty senior management, CEOs, and the board are getting reliable?"

Instead, they report discrete issues disconnected from enterprise survival and success.

#### *12.2.3 Politics Filter What Gets Audited*

Audits of sensitive or politically dangerous areas get postponed, narrowed, or reframed.

#### *12.2.4 Duplication Masks Blind Spots*

Multiple functions test the same low-value controls while ignoring mission-critical systems.

#### *12.2.5 Boards Receive Inputs, Not Conclusions*

Boards see dozens of micro-assurance artefacts but rarely a clear answer:

> *"Can we trust the risk/uncertainty information linked to this MCO?"; and that's assuming the board is getting any direct information on risk/ uncertainty linked to specific MCOs.*

IOCA exists to provide that answer.

### 12.3 The IOCA Model: A Structural Shift

IOCA reorganizes all assurance activities around the enterprise's MCOs.

The model consists of **five components**:

1. **Assurance Purpose**
2. **Assurance Scope (MCO-linked)**
3. **Assurance Integration Mechanisms**
4. **Assurance Output**
5. **Assurance Governance**

Together, these create a closed-loop system that produces objective-centric confidence—not siloed comfort.

### 12.4 Component 1: Assurance Purpose

Today, each assurance function has its own purpose:

audit → internal controls—report what internal audit sees as management's deficiencies/weaknesses on topics/things audit believes it is allowed to cover

risk → risk registers/risk heatmaps divorced from MCOs and performance
compliance → rules/regulations/laws
external audit → binary opinions on financial statements and financial statement internal controls

IOCA redefines them under a **single, unifying purpose**:

*Provide independent, evidence-based assurance on the reliability of risk/uncertainty and performance information relating to each Mission-Critical Objective.*

This aligns all assurance activity to PDG and OCRUM.

### 12.5 Component 2: Assurance Scope—MCO-Centred Assurable Units

IOCA replaces process-based and control-based audit planning with an **objective-centric scope model**.
Each MCO becomes an *assurable unit*.

For each MCO, assurance can examine:

- current/past performance reporting reliability
- uncertainty/risk assessment methods
- methods to identify and assess threats and opportunities
- AU/UU classification processes
- Risk treatments/controls linked to risks supporting the MCO
- culture, incentives, and escalation systems
- early warning indicator reliability
- management's declared confidence levels
- completeness and transparency of reporting

This shifts assurance from the **periphery** to the **core** of enterprise survival.

### 12.6 Component 3: Assurance Integration Mechanisms

IOCA eliminates duplication and blind spots through three mechanisms:

#### *12.6.1 The Integrated Assurance Map (IAM)*

A single map that shows, for each MCO:

- what is being assured
- by whom
- frequency
- depth
- assurance gaps
- duplication
- priority

It becomes the board's transparency tool.

#### *12.6.2 The Assurance Coordination Council (ACC)*

A cross-functional council composed of:

- Chief Audit Executive
- Chief Risk Officer
- Chief Compliance Officer
- Safety/Quality leads
- External audit liaison
- Key operational leaders

The ACC ensures:

- no duplication
- aligned timing
- consistent methods
- shared insights
- escalation integrity
- joint reporting on mission-critical issues

#### *12.6.3 Unified Assurance Standards*

Common definitions for:

- MCOs
- risk

- risk treatments
- uncertainty
- materiality
- evidence
- confidence/assurance
- findings
- ratings
- escalation triggers

This creates consistency across functions.

### 12.7 Component 4: Assurance Output—From Findings to Confidence

Traditional assurance produces **risk lists and audit findings.**

IOCA produces **confidence.**

The output of IOCA for each MCO includes the following.

#### *12.7.1 MCO Data Assurance Opinion*

Three possible sample ratings for each MCO:

1. **High Assurance**
2. **Moderate/Qualified Assurance**
3. **Low Assurance (Alert)**

#### *12.7.2 Assurance Confidence Score*

Integrated into the Board Assurance Index (BAI) attached to each MCO report.

#### *12.7.3 Summary of Assurance Evidence*

- data quality
- methodology quality
- completeness of reporting
- culture and escalation integrity
- early warning signal validity
- candid disclosure gets positive reports

#### *12.7.4 Gaps That Threaten MCO Achievement*

Direct linkage of assurance gaps to reliability of MCO risk/uncertainty reports.

#### *12.7.5 Recommended Management/Board Actions*

Specific, actionable oversight guidance and options.

This converts assurance from noise into governance fuel.

## 12.8 Component 5: Assurance Governance

The board must govern assurance, not merely receive it.

IOCA equips the board with:

- an **Assurance Charter** tied to board purpose
- an **MCO-based assurance plan**
- an **Assurance Performance Scorecard**
- direct linkage between assurance and compensation
- oversight of cultural factors that compromise assurance integrity

This creates a governance system that is **proactive, purpose-aligned**, and **defensible**.

## 12.9 How IOCA Supports AU/UU and the BAI

#### *12.9.1 IOCA Validates Information Used for AU/UU Classifications*

Every AU/UU classification/decision is strengthened or challenged by assurance evidence.

#### *12.9.2 IOCA Determines BAI Scores*

BAI relies on MCO assurance coverage as one of its core dimensions.

IOCA provides that coverage systematically and transparently.

#### *12.9.3 IOCA Reveals Hidden Risk Velocity*

Integrated cultural, operational, and data assurance can reveal accelerating uncertainty before performance deteriorates.

#### *12.9.4 IOCA Prevents Governance Theatre*

Boards no longer confuse "lots of assurance activity", "internal audit reports on management's internal control deficiencies", and "risk lists" with real "assurance effectiveness." An effective assurance framework focuses on ensuring management and the board are receiving reliable information on MCO risk/uncertainty at the target level of risk assessment rigour to help them make better decisions and improve performance.

### 12.10 IOCA in Action: Three Examples

#### *12.10.1 Example 1: Financial Reporting Integrity (Universal MCO)*

IOCA integrates:

- disclosure line-item risk ranking (which disclosure line items/ F/S notes get the most attention/most rigorous risk assessment)
- risk identification and assessment
- internal controls/risk treatments testing
- current performance in terms of errors detected/near misses
- external audit evidence
- finance transformation assurance
- culture and escalation assessments
- scenario modelling reliability

BAI increases because assurance is unified.

#### *12.10.2 Example 2: Safety in Aviation and Healthcare*

IOCA integrates:

- incident reporting systems
- risk identification and assessment
- safety culture metrics
- engineering or clinical assurance
- compliance checks
- operational risk assessments

MCO uncertainty becomes transparent—no filtering.

### *12.10.3 Example 3: Cybersecurity and Data Integrity*

IOCA knits together:

- risk identification and assessment
- IT controls/risk treatments audit
- threat monitoring
- penetration testing
- scenario modelling
- privacy compliance
- risk analytics
- culture (phishing/behaviour metrics)

The board receives a single consolidated "Cyber MCO Risk/ Uncertainty Status Assurance Opinion." The assurance opinion may mean there is high confidence management is accepting, and disclosing upwards, high levels of cyber risk and potential consequences.

## 12.11 Why IOCA Creates Board-Level Assurance Confidence

### *12.11.1 It Makes Assurance on MCO Risk/ Uncertainty Status Mission-Critical*

Assurance becomes a core pillar of purpose-driven governance.

### *12.11.2 It Focuses Assurance on Enterprise Survival*

No more "petty internal audit findings" and colour-coded risks divorced from MCOs and performance—the focus shifts to existential truth.

### *12.11.3 It Creates a Defensible Oversight Trail*

Courts and regulators can see clear evidence of structured, integrated oversight.

### *12.11.4 It Restores Board Trust in the Information System*

PDG's greatest gift is restoring decision making information integrity.

IOCA is the mechanism that makes this real.

### 12.12 Conclusion: Assurance Must Serve Purpose, Not Itself

When assurance is fragmented, the board receives comfort, not confidence.

When assurance is integrated, objective-centric, and tied to MCOs, the board receives:

- reliability
- transparency
- alerts re management filtering/withholding information
- early warnings
- cultural insight
- quantification of uncertainty
- evidence/explanations for AU/UU ratings
- inputs to the BAI

IOCA transforms assurance from a bureaucratic function into a strategic governance system.

In the next chapter, we turn to the **technology, analytics, and real-time reporting infrastructure** that makes PDG, OCRUM, AU/UU, BAI, and IOCA operational in the digital era.

# 13

# Implementing Purpose-Driven Governance

## From Blueprint to Boardroom Reality

*Blueprints and codes don't transform governance. Implementation does.*

### 13.1 Introduction: The Shift from Understanding to Action

The previous chapters built the intellectual foundation for Purpose-Driven Governance (PDG) and Objective-Centric Risk & Uncertainty Management (OCRUM). But knowing the architecture is not the same as installing it. Governance transformation requires a structured, staged implementation approach—one that addresses culture, infrastructure, incentives, information flows, and management/CEO/board human behaviour.

Most governance reform fails because it is treated as a tweaking exercise on status quo methods rather than a **system rebuild**. PDG requires more:

**a deliberate, engineered implementation roadmap that moves management and boards from awareness to continuous mission critical learning.**

This chapter provides that roadmap—five phases that take PDG from theory to boardroom reality.

DOI: 10.1201/9781003685753-17

**Phase 1: Awareness and Alignment**

## 13.2 Creating the Conditions for Transformation

PDG implementation begins with understanding—shared understanding. Boards and executives often believe they already have:

- Clear purpose;
- a functioning risk and controls management system;
- adequate assurance; and
- an effective reporting ecosystem.

They rarely do.

### *13.2.1 Step 1: Leadership Briefing*

If a company's culture allows it, a short session for directors and senior executives covering:

- the Quadrillion-Dollar Problem;
- don't tell/don't ask governance syndrome;
- the Failure Information Loop;
- Caremark/board fiduciary duty of care expectations;
- the PDG and OCRUM frameworks; and
- business case for change.

AUTHOR WARNING: Four decades of global experience and two years of intensive AI research indicate the majority of companies today lack cultures capable of supporting purpose driven governance and objective centric risk and uncertainty management. They have Don't Tell/Don't Ask Governance Syndrome. For those companies I advise CROs and CAEs to seek written confirmation if they aren't allowed to assess/report on mission critical objectives/risk, and provide clarity in charters and disclosures on what they are allowed to cover/report on to manage their personal liability/reputation risk.

### *13.2.2 Step 2: Diagnostic Assessment*

A PDG Diagnostic evaluates current state maturity across:

- board purpose clarity;
- MCO definition and oversight;

- uncertainty/risk status quantification;
- assurance fragmentation;
- culture and escalation integrity;
- board reporting; and
- alignment with UK Code 2024, King IV/V, and 1995 CoCo Canada. (NOTE: CoCo, unlike COSO internal control framework, puts high importance on PURPOSE and COMMITMENT alignment.

#### *13.2.3 Step 3: Governance Alignment Discussion*

Directors and the CEO must align on the need for change and the risks of sticking with status quo board oversight practices.

Completion of Phase 1 may, or may not, result in:

✓ recognition of structural oversight gaps
✓ unified will to proceed
✓ high-level sponsor commitment from CEO and board chair

Alternatively, the significant barriers that come with Don't Tell/Don't Ask Governance Syndrome may make it very clear—sticking with status quo governance practices, including risk list ERM and reporting management's internal control deficiencies in isolation from MCOs and performance, is the safer route for CROs and CAEs in those companies. If a company has DT/DA GS, it is highly unlikely that a move to mission critical/objective centric ERM and internal audit will BE ALLOWED/SUPPORTED without major regulatory and/or board intervention.

## Phase 2: Architecture and Infrastructure Design

### 13.3 Designing the PDG Governance System

This phase translates the PDG blueprint into tangible documents, structures, and workflows.

#### *13.3.1 Step 1: Draft and Approve Board Purpose Statement*

(Chapter 9)

This becomes the anchor for all subsequent design.

### *13.3.2 Step 2: Identify and Approve Mission-Critical Objectives (MCOs)*

(Chapter 10)

Including value-preservation and value-creation objectives.

### *13.3.3 Step 3: Build the MCOs Register*

- Each MCO internally defined
- MCO "OWNER/SPONSORs" defined/agreed
- MCOs and MCO OWNER/SPONSORS agreed with board
- Target risk/uncertainty risk assessment rigour assigned for each MCO
- Target assurance level on MCO risk/uncertainty status reports to CEO and board and who will provide that assurance, if any.
- Board reporting frequency

### *13.3.4 Step 4: Establish AU/UU and BAI Frameworks*

(Chapter 11)

- Thresholds documented
- Scoring criteria agreed
- Staff trained (note: this is a key step as most risk and internal audit staff have little or no experience doing objective centric risk/uncertainty status assessments)
- Reporting templates designed

### *13.3.5 Step 5: Design the IOCA Model*

(Chapter 12)

- Integrated Assurance Map
- Assurance Coordination Council
- Unified methodologies
- MCO Assurance Opinions

#### *13.3.6 Step 6: Update Governance Documentation*

- Board charters reflect purpose not just activities
- Committee charters
- Delegation of authority
- MCO risk/uncertainty management policy
- Risk and internal audit purpose mandates
- Strategy development protocols
- CEO reporting expectations

By the end of Phase 2, the governance architecture is defined—even if not yet operational.

**Phase 3: Pilot Implementation**

### 13.4 Running a Controlled Prototype before Full Rollout

Organizations dramatically increase implementation success by piloting PDG on **one to three MCOs** before scaling.

#### *13.4.1 Step 1: Select Pilot MCOs*

Typically:

- Top strategic/value creation objective,
- financial reporting integrity,
- safety/product/quality/customer service objective,
- Legal compliance with statutes with major consequences,
- cybersecurity/data integrity objective.

#### *13.4.2 Step 2: Build Pilot MCO Dashboards*

- owner/sponsors
- performance indicators/data
- AU/four-level UU classification
- BAI targets and scoring using target risk assessment rigour and target assurance levels
- Assurance providers
- Assurance commentary/opinions
- colour-agnostic visual clarity

#### *13.4.3 Step 3: Establish Reporting Rhythm*

Pilot teams report to the board or committee using Uncertainty Statusline dashboard and template. Detailed specs are available from the author to develop software to support PDG and OCRUM.

#### *13.4.4 Step 4: Conduct the First Integrated Assurance Review*

IOCA functions jointly assess reliability of pilot MCO reporting.

#### *13.4.5 Step 5: Conduct a Board-Level Pilot Review*

Board evaluates:

- usability of MCO dashboards
- clarity of MCO uncertainty/risk status
- reliability of BAI
- adequacy of board assurance
- quality of escalation
- behavioural changes in management reporting

This iterative cycle refines and stabilizes the model before enterprise-wide adoption.

**Phase 4: Enterprise Rollout**

### 13.5 Moving from Pilot to Full Implementation

The rollout phase applies PDG and OCRUM across all MCOs.

#### *13.5.1 Step 1: Scale the MCO Register*

Approve final starting point MCO list (typically 10–15).

Add owner/sponsors, target risk/uncertainty assessment rigour, target assurance level, and reporting frequencies.

#### *13.5.2 Step 2: Roll Out AU/UU and BAI*

Train all contributing teams.

Implement thresholds and scoring validation procedures.

### *13.5.3 Step 3: Deploy Integrated Reporting Infrastructure*

Technology support may include:

- MCO dashboards with direct link to full assessments
- MCO risk/uncertainty assessments and status data
- real-time early warning systems
- automated escalation alerts
- integrated assurance platforms
- digital audit trails

### *13.5.4 Step 4: Expand IOCA across All Functions*

- align risk and internal audit plans to MCOs
- link assurance testing to MCOs' risk/uncertainty status reports
- integrate external audit findings
- include culture diagnostics
- adopt unified assurance standards

### *13.5.5 Step 5: Redesign Board and Committee Agendas*

Every meeting becomes MCO-centred:

- MCO performance
- MCO uncertainty/risk status
- MCO risk/uncertainty status assurance, if any, on data
- MCO assurance reports
- CEO/board decisions required
- follow-up

### *13.5.6 Step 6: Incentive and Culture Alignment*

PDG requires risk-adjusted performance measures:

- executive compensation tied to MCO achievement and reliability of uncertainty status reports (e.g. consequences for reliable/unreliable MCO risk/uncertainty status reports)
- cultural indicators included in scorecards
- early-warning behaviours rewarded

- filtering punished, including CEO filtering if anyone is willing to report on that

This is where governance transformation becomes behavioural transformation.

**Phase 5: Continuous Learning and Global Alignment**

### 13.6 Creating a Self-Correcting Governance System

PDG is not a one-time installation.

It becomes a self-renewing capability.

#### *13.6.1 Step 1: Annual MCO Review*

Validate:

- relevance of MCOs to entity purpose/value creation/value preservation
- risk/uncertainty MCO status changes
- new MCO candidates
- regulatory updates on their enforcement focus
- lessons learned

#### *13.6.2 Step 2: Annual AU/UU and BAI Calibration.*

Update thresholds as confidence in the system increases.

#### *13.6.3 Step 3: Annual Integrated Assurance Opinion*

The board receives a unified, enterprise-level opinion on MCO risk/uncertainty/performance reporting reliability.

#### *13.6.4 Step 4: Board Purpose Evaluation*

Consistent with PDG principles and COSO and CoCo Canada's emphasis on monitoring.

#### *13.6.5 Step 5: Global Governance Code Alignment1*

PDG aligns with and strengthens major frameworks:
**UK Corporate Governance Code 2024**

- Clearer articulation of board responsibilities
- MCOs support new section 29 "internal controls effectiveness" expectations and aligns it with ERM
- IOCA strengthens disclosure credibility
- AU/UU + BAI enhance viability reporting
- Fixes fundamental flaw in section 28 calling for lists of "principle risks."

**King IV and emerging King V**

- Outcomes-based governance directly aligns with MCO framing
- Stakeholder-centric purpose aligns with PDG
- Integrated assurance maps reflect King IV's "three lines with integration" concept

**CoCo Canada 1995 (NOTE: 9 risk treatment principles developed by the author shown in 10.4 draw heavily on CoCo for key categories)**

- PDG operationalizes CoCo's "criteria of control" principles: purpose, commitment, capability, monitoring.
- IOCA becomes the practical realization of CoCo's control criteria.
- AU/four-level UU and BAI embed CoCo's emphasis on information reliability

PDG does not replace these frameworks. It **activates and actualizes** them.

#### *13.6.6 Step 6: Continuous Learning and Capability Building*

- annual PDG/OCRUM training
- scenario simulations
- inter-MCO stress testing
- culture and speak-up analysis
- cross-industry benchmarking

The governance system improves yearly—like a living, learning organism.

## 13.7 Why PDG Implementation Succeeds Where Traditional Reform Fails

### *13.7.1 It Focuses on Behaviour, Not Paperwork*

Boards change how they oversee, challenge, and decide.

### *13.7.2 It Activates Purpose*

Purpose becomes a governance rudder—not a slogan.

### *13.7.3 It Centres Oversight on What Actually Matters*

MCO orientation removes noise and blind spots.

### *13.7.4 It Creates Quantification and Evidence*

AU/UU and BAI transform uncertainty into actionable insight.

### *13.7.5 It Eliminates Fragmented Assurance*

IOCA integrates and aligns all assurance activities.

### *13.7.6 It Rebuilds Trust in Information Flows*

Filtering collapses; the truth moves upward.

## 13.8 Conclusion: From Blueprint to Reality

PDG implementation is not an incremental upgrade. It is the practical reconstruction of board oversight around purpose, mission-critical outcomes, quantified uncertainty, and verified information on MCO risk/uncertainty status and performance.

Organizations that implement PDG:

- see reality earlier;
- respond faster;
- increase management engagement;
- build trust with stakeholders;
- reduce legal exposure;
- increases board engagement;
- strengthen culture;, and
- create sustainable performance.

Organizations that do not remain captive to **the Purpose Void, Mission-Critical Blindness, the Failure Information Loop, and Don't Tell/Don't Ask.**

The remaining chapters will show how PDG scales globally; how it transforms investor expectations; and how boards can become early adopters in a new era of governance accountability.

## Note

1 AUTHOR NOTE: COSO's internal control framework is not covered here. The author believes there are a number of fatal flaws in it. COSO internal control framework was initially developed in the early 90s. The 2013 "update" did little to address the major flaws in the original "auditor centric" framework. Defining and communicating entity purpose and key objectives was rejected by COSO authors as a core element of an integrated control framework. COSO does not emphasize importance of performance data as a control. COSO ERM 2017 is now approaching a decade old and integrates with really old seriously flawed COSO internal control framework. There are no plans to address it. COSO/NACD governance guidance issued in draft in May 2025 was rescinded with no real explanation provided.

# PART V

# The Cultural Transformation

## Leadership, Courage, and Accountability

# 14

# Leading the Shift

## From Compliance to Confidence

*Systems create structure. Leaders create culture. The right combination creates confidence.*

### 14.1 Introduction: Why Leadership Behaviour and Support Determines PDG Success

Purpose-Driven Governance (PDG) provides the architecture.

OCRUM provides the analytical engine.

IOCA provides the assurance scaffolding.

But none of these systems can function without **leaders who model the behaviours that make truth flow upward**. Most companies today don't have frameworks that ensures truth on MCO risk/uncertainty status flows upwards, often with the support of their boards. (See endnote[1] for two simple questions every board could ask CEOs but most don't.)

Boards, CEOs, CROs, CAEs, and senior executives must adopt a new way of thinking and interacting—one that replaces the compliance mindset with **confidence-building behaviours**.

PDG depends on four leadership habits:

1. **Curiosity**—a relentless search for truth
2. **Candour**—the courage to speak the truth
3. **Collaboration**—breaking functional silos
4. **Consequence**—ensuring words and actions align

These behaviours interrupt and reverse the Don't Tell/Don't Ask Syndrome.

DOI: 10.1201/9781003685753-19 

This chapter explains the psychology behind them and offers practical tools for embedding them into the governance system.

## 14.2 Why Governance Fails: The Psychology behind Silence

Governance collapses not because leaders lack intelligence or expertise, but because they are subject to universal human dynamics.

### *14.2.1 Confirmation Bias*

Leaders unconsciously seek information that reinforces their beliefs.

### *14.2.2 Optimism Bias*

Executives, especially high performers, underestimate downside uncertainty and overestimate control.

### *14.2.3 Authority Gradient*

People filter truth when speaking to someone with more power.

### *14.2.4 Social Conformity (Asch Effect[2])*

Directors and executives conform to group consensus—even when they know the group is wrong.

### *14.2.5 Fear of Consequence*

Whistleblowers and truth-tellers fear retaliation; information is shaped for emotional safety.

PDG must override these tendencies with structured behaviour and deliberate leadership practice.

## 14.3 The Four Leadership Behaviours That Sustain PDG

### *14.3.1 Behaviour 1: Curiosity—The Antidote to Blind Certainty*

Curiosity is not a personality trait—it is a governance discipline.

A curious board asks:

- "What big assumptions are we making?"
- "Where could we be wrong?"
- "What risks/uncertainties are we not seeing?"
- "What worries you that we haven't discussed?"
- "If this fails, why will it fail?"

**Why Curiosity Matters**

Curiosity interrupts the Failure Information Loop.

It signals to management: **"We value truth, not comfort."**

**Practical Methods**

- "Red team" challenges at every board meeting
- Directors rotate as "designated sceptic"
- MCO spotlight sessions with independent experts
- Scenario analysis built into pre-read materials
- Mandatory uncertainty workshops during strategy cycles

Curiosity transforms oversight from ceremonial to investigative.

#### *14.3.2 Behaviour 2: Candour—The Courage to Name Reality*

PDG cannot survive without candour—from management *and* from the board.

Candour is the opposite of political filtering.

**Why Candour Matters**

Without candour, the AU/UU classifications, BAI scores, and MCO dashboards become meaningless—performative rather than evidence-based.

**Practical Methods**

- Establish "truth norms" for board discussions
- CEO and CRO required to declare BAI confidence levels on MCO reports out loud
- Internal audit empowered to report on MCO risk/uncertainty status reports and cultural risk directly to the board

- Anonymous cultural pulse checks tied to MCOs
- Directors required to disclose concerns in writing when dissenting

Candour is contagious. Silence is too.
Boards must choose which culture they create.

### *14.3.3 Behaviour 3: Collaboration—Integration of Roles, Not Duplication*

Collaboration is not friendliness.

It is **structural interdependence** among roles previously isolated:

- Board ↔ CEO
- CEO ↔ CRO
- CRO ↔ CAE
- Internal Audit ↔ Compliance ↔ Risk ↔ Safety
- Management ↔ Board Committees

**Why Collaboration Matters**

PDG requires integrated data, unified assurance, and shared visibility of MCO uncertainty/risk and performance.

Siloed actors create inconsistent truth.

**Practical Methods**

- Joint IA–Risk–Compliance planning through IOCA
- Integrated reporting packages tied to MCOs
- Cross-functional risk and assurance councils
- Shared incentive structures for early warning behaviours
- Regular "MCO Collaboration Labs" involving all assurance contributors

Collaboration is a design requirement, not a soft skill.

### *14.3.4 Behaviour 4: Consequence—Aligning Incentives with Truth*

Nothing drives culture more powerfully than consequences—what gets rewarded, what gets penalized, and what gets ignored.

**Why Consequence Matters**

Systems fail when there are no consequences for:

- withholding bad news;
- delaying escalation;
- sanitizing reporting;
- ignoring early warning indicators; or
- not challenging assumptions.

**Practical Methods**

- Executive compensation tied to MCO achievement and cultural indicators.
- CRO and CAE performance evaluated on MCO risk/uncertainty status information reliability and usefulness for decisions and performance improvement, not volume/activities completed.
- "Truth-telling behaviours" rewarded in scorecards.
- Disciplinary action for suppressing red flags.
- Board evaluation criteria aligned to PDG execution.
- CEO performance review includes the quality of MCO reporting.

Consequences shape culture faster than policies.

## 14.4 The Leadership Mandates of the Board, CEO, CRO, and CAE

Each leadership role must model PDG in a different way.

### *14.4.1 The Board's Mandate: Lead with Purpose and Demand Evidence*

Boards must:

- define board purpose;
- approve and monitor MCOs;
- insist on quantification/clarity in MCOs uncertainty status reports;
- challenge assumptions and narratives;

- protect whistleblowers and truth-tellers;
- require assurance on information reliability; and
- enforce MCO risk/uncertainty status reporting and BAI target rigour.

The board sets the cultural tone for **what the truth is allowed to look like.**

### *14.4.2 The CEO's Mandate: Enable Truth, Not Image*

CEOs must:

- model vulnerability and candour;
- remove political filtering;
- support early escalation;
- empower the CRO, CAE, and risk and internal audit teams;
- treat AU/UU alerts as assets, not threats;
- encourage dissent;
- reward transparency; and
- accept "bad news early" as a leadership virtue.

The CEO is the pivotal actor in collapsing Don't Tell/Don't Ask—when they are willing.

### *14.4.3 The CRO's Mandate: Become the Broker of Uncertainty*

CROs must evolve from risk-register custodians to:

- interpreters of/advisors on MCO uncertainty/risk status;
- integrators of data;
- challengers of assumptions;
- quantifiers of data sets used to make AU/UU decisions;
- advisors re how best to move from UU to AU;
- contributors to the BAI;
- partners in culture diagnostics; and
- drivers of early-warning systems.

OCRUM makes the CRO a strategic role, not the compliance role it is today in majority of organizations.

#### *14.4.4 The CAE's Mandate: Provide Assurance on Truth, Not Internal Controls*

Internal audit must shift from:

- internal control/compliance policing to
- **assuring the reliability of MCO risk/uncertainty status reporting.**

CAE responsibilities include:

- evaluating MCO risk/uncertainty status data reliability;
- testing AU/UN ratings escalation integrity;
- assessing cultural risk to MCO risk/uncertainty status reliability;
- issuing MCO Assurance Opinions under IOCA; and
- feeding evidence into the BAI for each MCO.

For many CAEs accustomed to opining whether they/internal audit likes/dislikes internal controls linked to areas/topics they believe they are allowed to cover, this is a massive paradigm shift—a paradigm shift that PDG makes both necessary and achievable.

### 14.5 Embedding the New Behaviours: Practical Methods

Behavioural transformation must be engineered.

Below are **eight practical tools** that embed PDG behaviours into daily governance.

#### *14.5.1 Tool 1: The PDG Behavioural Contract*

A short statement signed by directors and executives committing to:

- curiosity
- candour
- collaboration
- consequence
- courage
- timely escalation
- evidence-based oversight

It becomes part of annual evaluation.

#### *14.5.2 Tool 2: MCO Behavioural Indicators*

For each MCO, define behavioural metrics such as:

- risk/uncertainty status escalation speed
- frequency of dissent
- quality of early warnings
- transparency of data limitations
- culture pulse scores

Behaviours become measurable.

#### *14.5.3 Tool 3: The "Fifth Question" Protocol*

For every MCO deep dive, directors must ask:

*What are we pretending not to know?*

This question disrupts denial, groupthink, and premature certainty.

#### *14.5.4 Tool 4: Controlled Challenge Sessions*

Short, structured challenge MCO AU/UU ratings led by:

- independent experts
- cross-functional panels
- red teams
- dissent-designated directors

This formalizes healthy challenge.

#### *14.5.5 Tool 5: Transparency Pathways*

Anonymous and named reporting channels aligned to MCOs.
Data feeds directly into AU/UU and BAI.

#### *14.5.6 Tool 6: Boardroom Psychological Safety Design*

Deliberate interventions:

- rotating chairs
- time-boxed dissent

- "speak last" rules for the CEO
- pre-meeting dissent placeholders
- anonymous first-round polling

Psychological safety is engineered, not accidental.

#### *14.5.7 Tool 7: Incentive Rewiring*

Reward:

- early warnings
- transparency
- challenge
- cross-functional collaboration
- accuracy in MCO uncertainty/risk assessments

Penalize:

- withholding information
- distortion
- sanitization
- political filtering

#### *14.5.8 Tool 8: Story Reversal Technique*

Executives must periodically present:

> *The story we would tell if this MCO were failing.*

This reverses optimism bias and enables earlier detection of drift.

### 14.6 How These Behaviours Create a True Oversight Culture

When curiosity, candour, collaboration, and consequence operate together:

- MCO truth rises
- blind spots shrink
- filtering collapses
- AU/UU discussions become real

- BAI scores become more accurate
- IOCA becomes more effective
- risk velocity is detected early
- decisions improve
- governance becomes evidence-based

This is the cultural operating system PDG requires.

### 14.7 Conclusion: Leadership Is the Multiplier

PDG provides the architecture.

OCRUM provides the analytical precision.

IOCA provides the assurance backbone.

But **leadership behaviour is the multiplier**—the force that determines whether PDG becomes:

- a living governance system, or
- another framework that dies in a binder.

Boards, CEOs, CROs, and CAEs must lead the shift from compliance to confidence by modelling new habits of curiosity, candour, collaboration, consequence and courage.

With these behaviours, PDG becomes unstoppable.

Without them, PDG becomes impossible.

The next chapter will examine how PDG reshapes investor expectations, regulatory approaches, and the global governance landscape—positioning early adopters as leaders in the evolution of 21st-century corporate oversight.

### Notes

1 See Guest Post: "Mission Critical": Director Liability Ticking Time Bomb, D&O Diary, December 2024 for two simple questions every board could ask their CEO but most haven't:

> QUESTION #1—What are the company's MISSION CRITICAL OBJECTIVES, our top strategic/value creation and value preservation objectives key to long term success?

QUESTION #2—Who will be providing the board with information on risk/uncertainty re likelihood of achieving them? www.dandodiary.com/2024/12/articles/corporate-governance/guest-post-mission-critical-director-liability-ticking-time-bomb/

2 The **Asch Effect** describes the powerful human tendency to **conform to a group's opinion even when the group is clearly wrong.** It comes from classic experiments in the 1950s by Solomon Asch, which showed that people will often abandon their own accurate judgment to avoid standing out or contradicting a unanimous group.

# 15

# From Risk Aversion to Purpose Courage

*Governance does not fail because leaders take too much risk. It fails because they take too little courage.*

## 15.1 Introduction: The Courage Deficit at the Top

Most governance reform has focused on reducing risk:

- more controls
- more risk lists
- more checklist compliance
- more reporting
- more inspectors/policing roles
- more committees
- more disclosure

Yet the greatest collapses of our time—Boeing, Wells Fargo, Wirecard, SVB, Volkswagen, Carillion—did not occur because leaders and boards took reckless risks.

They occurred because leaders **lacked the courage** to:

- seek and confront uncomfortable truths;
- escalate early warnings;
- challenge dominant narratives;
- break cultural silence;
- insist on mission-critical evidence; and
- act before certainty governance had failed arrived.

This chapter argues that **courage—not caution—is the missing virtue** in modern governance.

And it reframes courage as the ultimate fiduciary duty.


DOI: 10.1201/9781003685753-20

## 15.2 Why Risk Aversion Has Become a Boardroom Disease

Boards pride themselves on being conservative, prudent, and risk-aware.

But this posture often masks a deeper dysfunction: **risk aversion,** which expresses itself through:

### *15.2.1 Passive Oversight*

Directors accept sanitized management reporting because challenging it feels confrontational.

### *15.2.2 Deference to Management*

Deference masquerades as respect but often disguises avoidance.

### *15.2.3 Fear of Looking Uninformed*

Directors avoid probing questions for fear of appearing unprepared.

### *15.2.4 Group Harmony over Intellectual Honesty*

Boards suppress outlier opinions for the sake of collegiality.

### *15.2.5 Legalistic Mindsets*

Oversight is equated with "compliance with codes," not the courage to seek truth.

These behaviours may reduce personal discomfort, but they amplify organizational exposure.

**Risk aversion breeds Mission-Critical Blindness.**

## 15.3 The Moral and Informational Risks Boards Avoid

Traditional governance recognizes financial, operational, and compliance risks. Just not in the context of achieving Mission-Critical Objectives (MCOs).

But two far more dangerous categories are rarely discussed:

#### *15.3.1 Moral Risk*

The risk that the board *fails to act in accordance with fiduciary purpose*, even when board is technically compliant with required board activities.

Examples include:

- allowing strategy to drift while meeting formal deadlines;
- tolerating cultural toxicity because performance looks strong;
- avoiding difficult conversations with the CEO;
- not asking CRO and CAE for regular reports on uncertainty/risk linked to MCOs;
- ignoring whistleblower discomfort; and
- celebrating performance achieved through integrity erosion.

#### *15.3.2 Informational Risk*

The risk that the board *believes it is informed when it is not.*

This is the core risk at the heart of:

- Boeing's safety crisis
- Wells Fargo's fake accounts
- Wirecard's fraud
- SVB's interest-rate exposure[1]
- countless cultural failures

Purpose-Driven Governance (PDG) exists to eliminate informational risk, but this cannot occur without courage.

### 15.4 Courage as a Fiduciary Duty

Traditional fiduciary duty focuses on:

- duty of care
- duty of loyalty
- duty of good faith

PDG adds a fourth dimension:

**Duty of courage—the obligation to ask, challenge, escalate, and act even when it is uncomfortable or politically risky.**

This is not metaphorical courage. It is structural courage—expressed through behaviours and decisions that protect purpose.

## 15.5 The Four Faces of Purpose Courage

PDG identifies four expressions of courage required in modern governance.

### *15.5.1 Courage to See*

Boards must confront uncomfortable information, including:

- risk/uncertainty status linked to MCOs
- weak culture signals
- conflicting data
- low/declining board data reliability (low BAI scores)
- AU → UU transitions
- escalating red flags
- early signs of ethical drift

Courage to see is the antidote to the Don't Tell/Don't Ask Syndrome.

### *15.5.2 Courage to Ask*

Courage to ask is the discipline of inquiry:

- "What are we missing?"
- "Where/how could this fail?"
- "If we were wrong, how would we know?"
- "Who benefits from the current narrative?"
- "What is the worst truth we aren't hearing?"
- "Who will be reporting on risk/uncertainty status linked to MCOs?"

This is the behavioural engine of PDG. Without courageous questions, MCO dashboards become decor.

#### *15.5.3 Courage to Challenge*

Boards must challenge:

- decisions on MCOs selected by management;
- management assumptions;
- risk/uncertainty assessments/decisions/framing;
- why most risk/internal audit today that report to boards don't report on risk/uncertainty linked to MCOs;
- optimism bias;
- cultural explanations;
- sanitized reporting;
- political filtering; and
- status-quo thinking.

Challenge is not conflict. Challenge is **care in action**.

#### *15.5.4 Courage to Act*

Courage to act means:

- escalating when MCO uncertainty becomes seriously unacceptable (red UU);
- replacing leaders, including CEOs, if necessary, who suppress truth;
- stopping strategies that drift off purpose;
- demanding independent assurance on MCO risk/uncertainty status;
- rejecting narratives that hide reality; and
- rebalancing incentives that distort culture.

Courage to act is the ultimate fiduciary move.

### 15.6 The Psychology of Courage in Governance

Courage is not innate. It is cultivated through the following.

#### *15.6.1 Identity*

Directors who see themselves as *guardians of purpose* behave differently than those who see themselves as advisors or mentors.

#### *15.6.2 Norms*

If the board normalizes candour, dissent, and curiosity, courage becomes safer.

#### *15.6.3 Systems*

PDG builds courage into:

- Board Purpose Statements
- MCO risk/uncertainty status oversight cycles
- AU/UU classification and disclosure
- BAI scoring
- IOCA assurance
- MCO deep dives

Systems create psychological permission and safety.

#### *15.6.4 Rewards and Consequences*

Incentives drive courage.
So do consequences for silence.

### 15.7 How PDG Creates Courage by Design

PDG does not require heroism.
It requires **structural courage**, embedded through design:

#### *15.7.1 MCO-Based Reporting Removes Ambiguity*

Boards know exactly where courage is needed.

#### *15.7.2 AU/Four-Level UU Makes Threats Visible*

Acceptable and unacceptable uncertainty ratings sometime demand action, sometimes from the board when CEO/management's risk acceptance decisions don't align with the board's risk appetite/tolerance.

#### *15.7.3 BAI Exposes Possible Data Weakness*

Low assurance scores force courageous inquiry.

#### *15.7.4 IOCA Reveals the Truth behind the Truth*

Integrated assurance verifies (or challenges) management narratives on risk and performance.

#### *15.7.5 Cultural and Behavioural Indicators Highlight Drift*

Directors cannot ignore patterns of silence.

#### *15.7.6 Board Purpose Statement Creates Accountability*

Directors must act in accordance with their stated purpose—or explain why they didn't.

PDG operationalizes courage.

### 15.8 How Courage Transforms Each Leadership Role

#### *15.8.1 Directors*

- Demand inconvenient MCO evidence/truth
- Defend dissent
- Prioritize purpose over comfort

#### *15.8.2 CEO*

- Reward truth-telling
- Publicly embrace uncertainty management
- Treat red flags as strategic assets
- Supports PDG and OCRUM

#### *15.8.3 CRO*

- Surface emerging threats to MCO achievement early
- Challenge optimism bias

- Provides input on MCO choices/candidates
- Assert/challenge AU/UU boundaries and decisions
- Provide opinions on OCRUM reliability/opportunities to improve

#### *15.8.4 CAE*

- Report uncomfortable assurance findings about MCO risk/uncertainty status reports and BAI assurance scores
- Provides input on MCO choices/candidates
- Test escalation pathways
- Provide independent challenge when culture suppresses truth

Courage is the connective tissue of PDG.

### 15.9 Practical Tools to Strengthen Purpose Courage

The following are nine tools boards can implement immediately.

#### *15.9.1 The "Courage Agenda Item"*

Every meeting includes one designated topic requiring courageous questioning.

#### *15.9.2 The Pre-Mortem Exercise*

Boards imagine the MCO failing catastrophically and discuss why.

#### *15.9.3 Confidential First-Round Polling*

Directors privately record concerns before group influence begins.

#### *15.9.4 The Escalation Integrity Test*

Periodic audits of whether bad news travels upward without distortion.

#### *15.9.5 The "Truth Session"*

Management presents unvarnished data without interpretation.

#### *15.9.6 The MCO Courage Index*

Measures speed and quality of board actions in significant MCO UU states.

#### *15.9.7 The Red Team Rotation*

At each meeting, one director challenges assumptions by design.

#### *15.9.8 Voice-of-the-Truth Channels*

Anonymous culture and speak-up data tied directly to MCOs.

#### *15.9.9 Board Purpose Self-Evaluation*

Directors rate themselves on their courage to act in line with purpose.

### 15.10 Courage as the Ultimate Governance Advantage

Companies that embed purpose courage outperform because they:

- detect risk to MCOs earlier;
- respond faster;
- maintain healthier cultures;
- avoid catastrophic blind spots;
- build trust with regulators and investors;
- attract ethical talent;
- maintain strategic focus; and
- protect long-term enterprise value.

Courage is not simply a moral virtue—it is an economic asset.

### 15.11 Conclusion: Governance Courage Is a Choice

Boards have two paths:

- **the comfort path**, dominated by caution, silence, and filtered information; or
- **the courage path**, defined by purpose, evidence, candour, debate, action and decisions.

The comfort path preserves the appearance of control.

The courage path builds actual control.

The comfort path avoids conflict.

The courage path prevents catastrophe.

The comfort path sustains the Quadrillion-Dollar Problem.

The courage path solves it.

PDG calls leaders to a higher standard—one rooted not in fear of risk but in **courage to fulfil purpose**, confront truth, and protect the future.

Courage is not optional.

It is the essence of 21st-century board fiduciary duty of care investors/broader stakeholders are hoping and looking for.

## Note

1 For more details on informational risk see SVB and Credit Suisse: The Case for Strong First-Line Risk Governance, Professor Parveen Gupta, Tim Leech, Strategic Finance, July 2023: https://riskoversightsolutions.com/wp-content/uploads/2023/07/The-case-for-strong-first-line-risk-governance.pdf

# 16

# Barriers to Governance Transformation

## Why the System Fiercely Resists Change

### 16.1 Introduction: Transformation without Traction

For many decades, governance reform has followed a predictable cycle: a scandal erupts, policy makers respond, frameworks expand, checklists lengthen, and boards double down on the familiar. The result is *more governance work, not better governance outcomes.* Purpose-Driven Governance (PDG) and Objective-Centric Risk & Uncertainty Management (OCRUM) offer a structural alternative—one that courts, investors, and stakeholders increasingly expect—but organizations struggle to adopt.

This chapter identifies the systemic barriers that prevent transformation. These are not minor frictions—they are the deep-rooted forces that keep global governance practices anchored in a compliance era while operating in a rapid change/high uncertainty era.

### 16.2 The Seven Barriers That Keep Governance Stuck

#### *16.2.1 The Comfort of Compliance*

Boards and executives reliably drift to what feels safe: frameworks, checklists, internal control assessments, and risk lists/risk heat maps. These tools create the *illusion* of risk oversight without the *work* of understanding mission-critical uncertainty. Compliance is predictable, familiar, and defensible—which makes it a powerful barrier to change.


DOI: 10.1201/9781003685753-21

**Why it persists:**

- Regulators rarely penalize "too much compliance."
- Regulators often default to policing/compliance roles for risk and internal audit.
- Consultants and software companies sell what boards buy: control maturity, risk lists, and traditional internal audit focused on reporting what audit sees as management's internal control deficiencies.
- Directors prefer structured activity over ambiguous judgment.

### *16.2.2 Incentive Misalignment and Denial of Information Risk*

Executives resist objective-centric oversight because it exposes uncomfortable truths: performance shortfalls, flawed strategy assumptions, and potentially uncertainty/risk levels unacceptable to the board and/or potentially discoverable if things go badly wrong. Boards resist because genuine oversight introduces personal knowledge and accountability they would prefer to avoid.

**Symptoms:**

- MCO reporting, for those CEOs and board directors that understand it, is framed as "too big a change."
- CROs/CAEs are rewarded for low-friction assurance, not challenging insights on risk/uncertainty linked to MCOs.
- Management filters negative signals to protect compensation and reputation.
- CEO blocks attempts by CROs and/or CAEs to move to a focus on assessing/reporting on risk/uncertainty linked to MCOs.

### *16.2.3 The Structural Power of the Don't Tell/Don't Ask Syndrome*

The core governance flaw becomes self-reinforcing:

- **Management doesn't tell** boards what they don't expressly ask for.
- **Boards don't ask** for information that might force conflict, delay plans, or reveal weak oversight.

The result: **risk blindness is normalized.** PDG/OCRUM threatens the equilibrium by requiring both sides to surface mission-critical uncertainty transparently.

### *16.2.4 Fragmented Risk and Assurance Silos*

CRO, CAE, Compliance, ESG, and Strategy teams each own their own reporting universe. Each produces "assurance" that appears useful, but is disconnected from mission-critical decision-making. Integration threatens turf, budgets, and decades-old identity narratives.

**Typical resistance phrases:**

- "That's not my mandate."
- "The board hasn't asked for that."
- "Audit shouldn't report on risk to mission critical objectives."
- "Risk/internal audit isn't allowed to report on risk/uncertainty linked to MCOs."
- "Our institutes haven't endorsed focusing risk or internal audit on MCOs"

### *16.2.5 Director Skill Gaps and the Myth of the Omniscient Board*

Most directors—despite being experienced, competent leaders—do not have:

- experience quantifying/describing uncertainty key objectives will be achieved;
- training in objective-centric MCOs oversight; or
- systems to convert risk/uncertainty data into oversight decisions.

Yet status quo governance culture pressures directors to *act* omniscient, discouraging admissions of uncertainty and skill gaps.

**Result:** The boardroom becomes a theatre of confidence, not a marketplace of truth.

#### *16.2.6 Framework Lock-In and Institutional Inertia*

Global governance frameworks (COSO, ISO, NACD, IIA, risk institutes) rarely abandon old structures. They revise, extend, "modernize," and "enhance"—but seldom rethink. They define the governance mainstream, and boards absorb their logic. Challenging status quo governance practices is seen as "breaking ranks", something that comes with some very real and immediate negatives to IIA, risk institutes, and director institutes built on legacy methods.

PDG/OCRUM is a paradigm shift, not a version upgrade—which makes it hugely disruptive to institutions that define themselves as risk, internal audit, and governance standard-setters wed to status quo methods.

#### *16.2.7 Fear of Consequence (Legal, Political, and Personal)*

Directors and executives often perceive transparency about MCO uncertainty/risk as dangerous:

- It may reveal negligence.
- It may expose strategic weakness.
- It may create shareholder expectations.
- It may generate discoverable evidence in litigation.

Ironically, the emerging *Caremark 2.0* era punishes opacity more than candour. Business judgment rule protects directors that act in good faith—but the fear persists.

### 16.3 The Reinforcement Loop: How Barriers Keep Each Other Alive

The barriers do not operate independently—they reinforce one another in a self-stabilizing system:

- Compliance comfort reduces curiosity.
- Lack of curiosity enables Don't Tell/Don't Ask.
- Don't Tell/Don't Ask Governance Syndrome protects silos.
- Silos shield skill gaps.
- Skill gaps make directors dependent on flawed frameworks.
- Framework dependence discourages innovation.
- The fear of consequence discourages transparency.

The result: A governance system optimized *not* for performance, but for self-protection.

### 16.4 Breaking Through: What Makes Transformation Possible

Despite the massive and very real barriers to better corporate governance, transformation is possible and accelerating where three conditions align:

1. **A Catalyst Event**
   A governance failure, activist investor pressure, regulatory demand, or derivative litigation forces change beyond cosmetic reform.
2. **A Director or Executive Champion**
   One person—board chair, committee leader, CFO, CRO, CAE, or CEO—refuses to accept the status quo and demands purpose-centric/MCO-centric clarity.
3. **A Repeatable, Evidence-Based Method**
   PDG and OCRUM provide structure, tools, and metrics (MCO Register, AU/UU analysis, BAI, IOCA). Once the blueprint exists, governance begins behaving like engineering—not ritual. Logic overcomes comfort of governance rituals.

### 16.5 The Path Forward: From Barriers to Breakthroughs

The next chapter moves from assessing obstacles to better governance to imagining the long-term implications: a capitalism where transparency, purpose, and accountability converge. But recognition of the huge barriers to positive change is essential. Boards cannot transform what they cannot name. Even the best logic and business case often fail to overcome fierce attachment to/protection of corporate governance methods that have proven to be hugely ineffective countless times.

PDG does not fail because it is flawed; it fails because the status quo is powerful beyond what most people can imagine. Understanding the sources of that power to protect status quo governance, risk, and internal audit methods that don't work very well is the first step to better governance.

# 17

# The Future of Accountable Capitalism

## 17.1 Introduction: A System at a Crossroads

With the very real and daunting barriers to governance transformation now visible and named (Chapter 16), the final task is to look forward. Capitalism is entering an era where legitimacy is no longer guaranteed—trust must be earned through transparency, purpose, and demonstrable accountability. Stakeholders expect more than financial performance; they expect responsible stewardship of Mission-Critical Objectives (MCOs), honest reporting of uncertainty, and governance that protects the long-term viability of the enterprise.

Purpose-Driven Governance (PDG) and Objective-Centric Risk & Uncertainty Management (OCRUM) were designed not merely to fix corporate oversight and improve governance, but to support a new model of capitalism—one where boards lead with measurable purpose and where performance, risk, and assurance operate as integrated systems rather than disconnected functions.

## 17.2 The End of the Shareholder Primacy Era

For decades, governance operated under the implicit assumption that maximizing shareholder value—quarter by quarter—was the board's central purpose. This narrow view created predictable systemic distortions:

- short-termism in capital allocation
- blind spots around mission-critical uncertainty

DOI: 10.1201/9781003685753-22 

- incentives that discouraged transparency
- erosion of trust among employees, regulators, and society

In the emerging era, stakeholders (investors included) increasingly see governance through a different lens: **Does this board know, monitor, and protect the MCOs that determine long-term value and viability?** PDG reframes board purpose accordingly.

### 17.3 Courts and Regulators Are Quietly Re-Writing Expectations

Delaware's modern "Caremark 2.0" jurisprudence signals a profound shift:

Boards must proactively ensure systems exist to surface, escalate, and evaluate uncertainty linked to MCOs. Several themes now define the regulatory horizon:

1. **Oversight must be objective-centric, not activity-centric.** Boards will no longer satisfy courts by reviewing risk heat maps, internal audit plans and reports, or ESG dashboards that lack mission-critical risk specificity.
2. **Evidence of board engagement will matter.** Minutes, charters, agendas, and assurance reports will be evaluated not for volume, but for *relevance* to the company's top strategic/value creation and value preservation objectives.
3. **Directors must show good-faith questioning of management judgment.** The age of passive receipt of filtered information is ending. The expectation is shifting toward **informed curiosity, independent challenge, courage,** and **transparent follow-through**.

### 17.4 Why PDG/OCRUM Align with the Future of Oversight

#### *17.4.1 Purpose as a Measurable Governance Anchor*

Boards that explicitly define their purpose—Chapter 9's starting point—create a stable reference point for oversight decisions. In the next era of capitalism, unclear or implied but not stated purpose will increasingly be treated as a governance flaw.

#### *17.4.2 MCOs as the Organizing Framework*

Governance that does not anchor oversight of MCOs is governance that cannot meaningfully protect enterprise value. Chapter 10s method for defining MCOs will become standard practice in forward-looking organizations.

#### *17.4.3 Quantification of Uncertainty as a Fiduciary Responsibility*

Uncertainty quantification (Chapter 11) offers what traditional risk lists cannot:

a transparent, falsifiable, and comparable view of whether uncertainty is acceptable or not.

#### *17.4.4 Integrated Assurance as a New Competitive Advantage*

Chapter 12 introduced Integrated Objective-Centric Assurance (IOCA). Organizations that adopt it will exhibit fewer blind spots, lower assurance cost, and higher board confidence. The market will increasingly reward this model.

#### *17.4.5 Implementation Discipline and Continuous Learning*

Chapter 13s roadmap shifts governance from episodic reform to **structured transformation**. This discipline is required for capitalism to rebuild legitimacy.

### 17.5 The Market Rewards Entities with High Oversight Confidence

Capital markets, rating agencies, insurers, and institutional investors are evolving toward a new priority: **organizational resilience**.

Companies that can demonstrate:

- clear purpose
- well-defined MCOs
- transparent AU/UU uncertainty/risk thresholds
- a Board Assurance Index (BAI)
- integrated assurance across all major risk domains

will increasingly benefit from:

- lower cost of capital
- stronger insurer confidence
- higher investor/stakeholder trust
- reduced litigation exposure
- improved talent attraction and retention

Oversight confidence becomes a tangible asset.

### 17.6 Capitalism after Transparency: What the Future Looks Like

The long-term trajectory points to a governance environment where:

1. **Board purpose becomes a mandatory disclosure.**
   Regulators and/or investors will insist boards explicitly state whom they serve, how they define board success, and how they monitor it.
2. **Mission-critical uncertainty becomes auditable.**
   Financial statements and other value preservation areas will not be the only auditable representations. Boards will disclose how they monitor uncertainty linked to the objectives that determine corporate survival and success.
3. **Assurance shifts from comfort to accountability.**
   The old "three lines" model will be replaced by integrated "five lines of assurance"[1] tied to MCOs, not to organizational silos, annual/semi-annual risk lists, and internal audit plans.
4. **Stakeholder trust is earned through candour, not marketing.**
   Disclosing uncertainty will be a sign of strength, not weakness—as Chapter 15's concept of "Purpose Courage" becomes an expected board competency.
5. **Governance becomes a discipline of design, not reaction.**
   Framework-led governance gives way to architecture-led governance—purpose-driven, objective-centric, evidence-based.

## 17.7 A Global Call to Lead with Measurable Purpose

Capitalism's survival depends on boards willing to confront their most uncomfortable truth: **oversight without purpose is theatre**. Directors that act with courage must:

- demand clarity on MCOs;
- challenge management constructively;
- insist on transparency on MCO risk/uncertainty;
- evaluate performance against entity purpose and MCOs; and
- embrace courage as a fiduciary duty.

This is more than a governance reform. It is a redefinition of what it means to lead.

## 17.8 Conclusion: What the Next Era Requires

The future of accountable capitalism will be shaped not by regulators, courts, or frameworks—but by boards and companies that choose to govern differently. PDG and OCRUM offer the architecture, discipline, and tools required to move from symbolic ritualistic governance to **purpose-engineered governance**.

The Quadrillion-Dollar Question remains: **Will boards lead with purpose—or will they wait to be forced?**

The answer will define the legitimacy of capitalism for decades to come.

### Note

1 Three Lines of Defense vs Five Lines of Assurance: Elevating the Role of the Board and CEO in Risk Governance Tim Leech, Lauren Hanlon, 2016: https://riskoversightsolutions.com/wp-content/uploads/2020/06/3LoD-vs-5LoA-Elevating-the-Role-of-the-Board-and-CEO-May-31-2016-Risk-Oversight-Solutions-Inc.pdf

# Epilogue

## The Next Conversation

*The future of governance will not be written in hindsight. It will be shaped by foresight.*

The world is entering an era where information will no longer arrive in quarterly packets, carefully curated, delayed, and filtered through organizational politics. Artificial intelligence (AI), real-time analytics, digital assurance systems, and integrated data flows are rewriting what oversight can be—transforming governance from a retrospective exercise into a continuous capability.

For decades, boards have governed in the dark, relying on dashboards and report packets that summarize the past rather than illuminate the present. They have depended on trust, tone, and tradition rather than evidence, transparency, and truth. This book has argued for a fundamental shift—from compliance to confidence, from risk aversion to purpose courage, from siloed functions to integrated oversight, from sanitized narratives to quantified uncertainty.

But the greatest shift is still ahead.

### Continuous Oversight: The Coming Operating System of Governance

AI makes it possible for boards and executives to:

- detect emerging uncertainty weeks before humans notice patterns;
- monitor proposed and selected Mission-Critical Objectives (MCOs) in real time;
- flag cultural drift before it becomes misconduct;
- assess information reliability instantly;
- integrate assurance from multiple sources automatically;


DOI: 10.1201/9781003685753-23

- create transparent audit trails without human bottlenecks; and
- simulate future scenarios with unprecedented fidelity.

The tools of Purpose-Driven Governance (PDG)—Acceptable Uncertainty/four-level Unacceptable Uncertainty (AU/UN) classification, Board Assurance Index (BAI), integrated assurance, MCO dashboards—will soon be powered by real-time sensors, analytics engines, and intelligent monitoring systems that surface truth without delay, distortion, or fear to help management and boards make decisions and improve performance.

In this world, governance will no longer depend on who chooses to speak up.

It will depend on what the data reveals.

### AI as a Partner in Purpose

AI cannot replace judgement, courage, or accountability.

But it can enforce transparency, reduce informational risk/uncertainty, and protect integrity by:

- challenging optimistic assumptions;
- identifying inconsistencies across systems;
- surfacing contradictions in performance narratives;
- verifying data reliability at scale;
- reducing the burden of manual assurance tasks; and
- providing early-warning indicators tied to MCOs.

AI becomes not an overseer—but a **co-governor**: a relentless seeker of truth that helps boards see reality before it becomes crisis.

### From Episodic Oversight to Perpetual Insight

Future governance will be defined by:

- continuous learning instead of periodic reviews;
- proactive intervention instead of reactive justification;
- living forward looking dashboards instead of static reports; and
- evidence-rich decision-making instead of judgement by intuition.

Boards will no longer wait for failures to expose blind spots.

Blind spots will expose themselves.

### The Next Conversation

This book ends, but the conversation begins.

A conversation about:

- what it means for boards to work alongside intelligent systems;
- how continuous risk/uncertainty transparency linked to MCOs reshapes fiduciary duty;
- how assurance becomes digitized and democratized;
- how culture can be monitored through behaviour signals;
- how investors and regulators will respond to real-time governance; and
- how capitalism changes when purpose becomes measurable and oversight becomes instantaneous.

The question is no longer: **"Can boards govern better?"** They can.

The question is now: **"Are we ready to build governance that learns as fast as the world changes?"**

PDG provides the architecture. AI provides the velocity. Together, they offer a path toward a future where oversight is not an event, but a living system—transparent, adaptive, and aligned with entity and board purpose in every moment.

The next era of governance is emerging. May this book serve as your invitation—and your blueprint—for the conversation ahead.

# Glossary of Abbreviations

**Core Frameworks and Concepts**

**AU/UU** (Acceptable Uncertainty/Unacceptable Uncertainty): A classification framework for evaluating whether uncertainty levels linked to an objective are within board-approved tolerance.

**BAI** (Board Assurance Index): A structured rating (typically 1–5) reflecting the board's level of confidence in the reliability of information on MCO performance and uncertainty.

**DT/DA GS** (Don't Tell/Don't Ask Governance Syndrome): A systemic governance failure where management withholds critical information and boards fail to demand it.

**IOCA** (Integrated Objective-Centric Assurance): A model integrating internal audit, risk, compliance, and external assurance around MCOs to provide coherent, decision-relevant assurance.

**MCO(s)** (Mission-Critical Objective(s)): The small set of objectives essential to organizational survival, value creation, and value preservation.

**OCRUM** (Objective-Centric Risk & Uncertainty Management): A management and governance approach that assesses and manages uncertainty relative to specific objectives rather than standalone risk lists.

**PDG** (Purpose-Driven Governance): A governance model that anchors board oversight in explicitly defined purpose, mission-critical objectives, and linked risk/uncertainty and assurance.

### Governance, Risk, and Assurance Functions

**CAE** (Chief Audit Executive): Head of the internal audit function.

**CEO** (Chief Executive Officer): Senior executive accountable for overall management performance.

**CLO** (Chief Legal Officer): Executive responsible for legal and regulatory matters.

**CRO** (Chief Risk Officer): Executive responsible for risk management frameworks and reporting.

**ERM** (Enterprise Risk Management): Traditional frameworks and practices used to identify and manage risks, typically via risk registers and heat maps.

**IA** (Internal Audit): Independent assurance function traditionally focused on internal controls, compliance, and process effectiveness.

### Governance Standards, Frameworks, and Codes

**CoCo** (Criteria of Control (Canada)): Canadian framework focusing on control, purpose, and organizational effectiveness.

**COSO ERM** (Committee of Sponsoring Organizations Enterprise Risk Management Framework): Widely used US-based risk management framework emphasizing integration with strategy and performance.

**ISO 31000** (International Standard for Risk Management): Global standard defining risk as "the effect of uncertainty on objectives."

**ISO 37000** (Governance of Organizations Standard): International guidance on governance principles and practices.

**King IV / King V** (South African Corporate Governance Codes): Governance frameworks emphasizing stakeholder inclusivity and integrated thinking.

**OECD Principles** (G20/OECD Principles of Corporate Governance): Global benchmark principles for corporate governance.

**UK Code (2024)** (UK Corporate Governance Code 2024): UK regulatory framework outlining expectations for boards, including "principal risks."

### Legal, Regulatory, and Risk Terms

**AML** (Anti-Money Laundering): Regulatory framework to prevent financial crime.

**Caremark** (In Caremark International Inc. Derivative Litigation (1996)): Landmark case defining directors' duty to ensure oversight systems exist.

**CSRD** (Corporate Sustainability Reporting Directive): EU regulation requiring enhanced sustainability disclosures.

**D&O** (Directors and Officers (Liability Insurance)): Insurance protecting board members and executives from legal claims.

**DGCL** (Delaware General Corporation Law): Foundational corporate law governing many US companies.

**FCPA** (Foreign Corrupt Practices Act): US law addressing bribery and accounting transparency.

**SOX** (Sarbanes–Oxley Act): US legislation focused on financial reporting and internal controls.

### Performance, Risk, and Information Concepts

**Failure Information Loop**: A systemic cycle where fragmented, filtered, and sanitized information leads to ineffective board oversight.

**Information Asymmetry**: Gap between what management knows, what boards receive, and what stakeholders assume.

**KPI(s)** (Key Performance Indicator(s)): Metrics used to measure organizational performance.

**Mission-Critical Blindness**: The inability of boards to see and monitor risks linked to core objectives.

**Risk Heat Map:** Visual tool plotting likelihood vs. impact of risks (often criticized in the manuscript as misleading).

**Risk Register**: A traditional list of identified risks, often disconnected from objectives.

Emerging/Supporting Concepts in the Manuscript

**Checklist Governance**: Governance focused on compliance processes rather than outcomes.

**Closed-Loop Oversight System**: A governance system with continuous feedback: objectives → uncertainty → reporting → challenge → assurance → follow-up.

**Purpose Void**: The absence of a clearly defined board or governance purpose.

**Quadrillion-Dollar Question**: The central thesis: whether boards will oversee risk and uncertainty linked to mission-critical objectives.

For Product Safety Concerns and Information please contact our EU
representative GPSR@taylorandfrancis.com
Taylor & Francis Verlag GmbH, Kaufingerstraße 24, 80331 München, Germany

www.ingramcontent.com/pod-product-compliance
Ingram Content Group UK Ltd.
Pitfield, Milton Keynes, MK11 3LW, UK
UKHW020205200926
475702UK00004B/627
* 9 7 8 1 0 4 1 1 6 6 6 5 8 *